V

E

This book is due for return on or before the last date shown below.

Dreaming of success

Are you dedicated and determined
to reach the summit of your dreams
to grasp the goals set in your mind;

Consecrating your youth and energy
your sleep and your waken hours
to embrace the goals your imagine;

A strategic drive to desired success
through application a dividend earn
the attainment of your aspirations?

Writing the Medical CV

Effective professional communication

Sam McErin MSc MRCP MBA

mentor on communication skills

Edukom

www.edukom.co.uk

Edukom
5 Cambridge Close
Sale, Manchester
England M33 4YJ

www.edukom.co.uk
info@edukom.co.uk

First published by Edukom 2004
Copyright © Edukom 2004

ISBN 1-904836-01-1

Writing the medical CV

Contents

Preface

Writing the Medical CV is intended to help doctors who do not feel confident enough to write CV, letters and reports to enhance their professional careers.

A good CV improves a doctor's chances of getting interviews for clinical or managerial posts. Over the years I have watched bright, hard working doctors fail to get jobs they deserved simply because their CVs were not good enough to secure them interviews. Many got the posts when the CVs were improved. Effective writing is essential for success in clinical and managerial careers.

If I need a job I inform potential employers of my suitability and availability. I am careful with written communications (CVs, letters, reports, response to complaints, and e-mails). What do I want to say? What should I leave out? I write what I want to write– not less and not more. I think hard before applying for jobs. I examine posts and courses for immediate and future benefits. Will the post, will the course, advance my career?

It is essential that you learn to write effective letters, curricula vitae, research project and reports. Effective writing is essential to accessing opportunities and resources.

When you apply for a job, your aim is to convince the recruiter to pick you and not another doctor. Like a vendor, you display your wares to customers. Your qualifications, experience, skills, and personality– *YOU* are on sale. The best goods sell first. Similarly the best candidates are selected– hopefully. Your duty is to present yourself as the best available.

In a complex society you must be able to write, talk and listen well– that is *play the communication game effectively.* In a crowded socio-medical environment you must communicate effectively to get your story heard, to ensure your needs are met.

Your CV must grow with you (qualifications, teaching, clinical audits, research, publications, presentations, leadership, communication skills, etc).

Writing the Medical CV concentrates on written messages– letters, CVs and reports (clinical, legal, research, audit, and dissertations). It shows you how to present your qualifications, your clinical experience and skills (your CV) to maximise your chances of being called for an interview. It discusses the impact of impressions *(appearance, speech/language and disposition)* at interviews.

I have used my experience as a job seeker, clinician and a recruiter (short-listing and interviewing) to write this book. It explains and shows you how to:

- Write a winning CV
- Write effective letters
- Apply for jobs
- Manage interviews

- Grow (develop) your CV
- Execute a clinical audit
- Write a dissertation/thesis
- Write a research paper

The letters, CVs and individuals named in this book are fictitious. A few known institutions are used to maintain a sense of reality. Of course the stories are heavily influenced by my experience!

I hope **'Writing the Medical CV'** will help you build a rewarding career.

S McErin

Sam McErin

sammcerin@yahoo.co.uk

1.0 Writing effective letters

Writing effective letters

1.1 Why write?

Writing letters and reports is an important part of a doctor's professional life. So learn to write letters that do their jobs well– that say what you want to say; no more, no less.

My letters are usually brief. They have objectives and functions. I write to keep in touch with friends and relatives, and for business and professional purposes.

Your letter should say what you want it to say; no more, no less.
- think of what you are going to say and how you will say it
- write politely; there is no need to record your rudeness
- avoid ambiguity; your message should be understood clearly
- use clear simple words, avoid jargon wherever possible
- use short words, short sentences, and short paragraphs
- avoid superfluous professional jargon.

1.2 Do you have to write?

Letters are kept by individuals and definitely by business, government and educational organisations– at least for a while. They may be scanned and kept on computers. Do you want you letter on long-term record? Then make it clear, concise and precise.

When dealing with large organisations it is best to put your considered case in writing. However you must think carefully before writing. Draft your letter, read it and rewrite it till it says what you want it to say and nothing else. You may not be able to retract and amend it later.

A letter (including e-mail) may be used as evidence in court. It may support your case or be used against you.

Do you need to write that letter?

Have you talked with those involved? Can you get what you want without writing? If you should write (and often you must), then do it well.

1.3 Structure of a letter

A letter has several parts (writer's address, date of writing, recipient's name and address, a greeting, the message, a closing phrase, writer's signature and name, and in organisations, the writer's position): and each has a function.

1.3.1 The writer's address

This is where the reply would be sent. The address should include post-codes, zip codes and/ or post office box numbers as appropriate. The address may be:

the premises (private or public)– mail is brought to the building and put into a receptacle or handed to a receptionist [*Bank of England, Threadneedle Street, London EC2R 8AH*]; **or**

a post office box number and its location– mail is placed in numbered box at a post office to be collected by the recipient or his representative *[Bank of Uganda, PO Box 7120, Kampala, Uganda]*.

Telephone and fax numbers, and e-mail address

Organisations (health authorities, health care trusts, GP practices, etc) and many individuals include telephone and fax numbers and e-mail addresses on their letter-heads. Wise applicants too include adequate contact details in their CVs and letters of application.

Post codes and Zip codes

Delivering mail (letters, parcels) is facilitated by suffixes to address– *post codes (zip codes in USA)*. The combination of locality, letters and numerals helps in

the sorting and delivering of mail E.g.:
- Bank of England, Threadneedle Street, London **EC2R 8AH**.
- Microsoft Corporation, 1 Microsoft Way, Redmond **WA 98052-6399**.

EC2R 8AH is the format for post codes in Britain and *WA 98052 - 6399* is the style for *zip codes* in the USA.

If you do not provide a full address, you may not get a reply.

1.3.2 References

References (**Your Ref., Our Ref.**) are vital in business and official letters. They relate the letter to previous communications (what was done, ordered, agreed, refused, postponed, contracted or bought before*)*. They assist in retrieving files.

Official letters may also contain initials of the officer responsible for the letter and of the secretary who typed it– EBT/MS. These too assist in handling queries about the letter. *Who knows about this? Who made the decision?*

Order Number, Invoice Number

Business letters may also quote *Order Number,* or *Invoice Number,* when referring to orders and invoices for the purchase or sale of goods. The numbers are needed in the handling, dispatch and payment for goods. Their use speeds up business transactions. Quote them appropriately in your business letters and e-mails.

1.3.3 The date of writing

This fixes the letter in history. The date is important in business and legal transactions. When was the letter written? When was the order made, dispatched, or paid for? When was the promise or contract made?

1.3.4 The recipient's *(receiver's)* **name** and/or **official title**

The name of the recipient– individual or officer to whom the letter is directed (the receiver) – should be included. This speeds up official communications, ensuring that the letter goes straight to the right officer.

You should at least find out the title of the officer dealing with your inquiry, business, or subject of your interest. Do not write to huge organisations and hope that somebody will pass your letter to the right person. It may not happen.

Even when you know the officer's name, it is wise to include the official title. Your letter may arrive after that individual has left the post or gone on holiday. The deputy or successor will open official letters (if the office is indicated), but not what appears to be personal communications.

Common forms official titles
Examples of words/phrases used to start official letters are listed below:
- *Dear Sir, Dear Judge, The Hon. Mr. Justice* (high court judges)
- *The Clerk* (of the court, town, district, council
- *The Permanent Secretary* (government ministries)
- *The Manager* (bank, hotel, building society sporting teams, etc)
- *The Managing Director* (business company, parastatal body, quango, etc)
- *The Director* (bureau, centre, foundation, museum, gallery, etc.)
- *The Registrar* (births, deaths, marriages, tribunal, university, etc.)
- *The Dean* (diocese, university, academic faculties, diocese)
- *The Officer-in-Charge* (armed forces unit, police unit)
- *The Secretary* (commissions, foundations, committees, clubs, etc)
- *The President,* (republic, chambers of commerce, union, etc

1.3.5 The recipient's (receiver's) address
The residential or business postal address to which the letter is sent should also be included, particularly in business and official letters.

BMJ Bookshop	*The Medical Director*
BMA House	*Mulago Hospital*
Tavistock Square	*PO Box 7051*
London WC1H 9JR	*Kampala*
United Kingdom	*Uganda.*

Did I hear you say that you will write the address on the envelope? Envelopes are usually thrown away after removing the letter. So include the recipient's name and address on the letter too.

Personal letters often omit the receiver's address. It is better to include it unless you are writing to close friends and relatives. If you are not sure, include the recipient's (receiver's) address in your letter.

1.3.6 The greeting
A greeting is used to start a letter, to greet the receiver. It is pure and simple politeness, like saying *Good morning* to somebody when you don't care whether his morning is good or terrible.

*Dear Sir, Dear Madam, Dear Mr. Smith, Dear…*are typical phrases used to start letters. The word *Dear* does not mean the recipient is a loved friend or relative. Letters to enemies also start with *Dear….*

Recipient's title is not known
Official letters and publications in which the writer has not given her or his title—not indicated if he/she is a Mr, a Miss a Mrs, a Dr, nor given any other title or other form of address are becoming common. Many BMJ job adverts direct applicants to contact a "Sam Temps" in the medical staffing office or human resources department.

Is "Sam Temps" a Miss a Mrs or a Mr? How do you address "Sam Temps" in a letter? I do not like writing to Dear Sir/Madam when I know the recipient will be "Sam Temps". So my letter would start:

Sam Temps
St Luke's Hospital
33 Leicester Rd
Market Harborough LE16 7BN

Dear Sam Temps

Re: Application for post of specialist registrar in Medicine– Ref M23

1.3.7 Re: Subject:

Business and official letters should have headings to the body of the letter. This states the subject/issue/business of the letter. Headings may start with *Re:* (in the matter of) or with **Subject.**

> Re: *Application for the post of senior house officer*
> Subject: *Application for the post of senior house officer.*

In the past headings were underlined: Re: Financing study leave.
Nowadays headings are highlighted. **Re: Financing study leave**. Some letter writers are highlighting and underlining! Highlighting alone is enough.

The heading is useful in directing the letter to the individual dealing with the matter. Some organisations (and individuals) receive so much mail that untitled letters risk getting lost in paper piles.

Headings are helpful in sorting, filing and retrieving letters. So give your letter a clear, concise title. If you have thought about the purpose of your letter, formulating a heading will be easy.

1.3.8 The message

This is the reason for writing the letter. If you want somebody to understand and act on the basis of your letter, then give them the full picture. Write clearly and concisely, give enough facts and detail so that the reader gets your *message.*

So before you put pen to paper or fingers to computer keyboard, *think:*
• What would you want to know if you received such a letter?
• What do you want to say?
• What don't you want to say?
• How do you want to say it?

1.3.9 The closing phrase *(signing off)*

A friendly phrase is used to end letters. In business and official letters the closing phrase is usually one of the following:

Yours sincerely (if the letter started with a personal name)
Yours faithfully (if an official title only was used)
With regards (between colleagues of same rank)
Your obedient servant (officer to a senior; rarely used).

These phrases have nothing to do with sincerity, faithfulness (trust), obedience or servitude. They are simple historical remnants of English politeness, no more and no less. Polite letter writers use them.

Letters to relatives and close friends end with:
Your affectionate (daughter, son, etc.)
Your (brother, son, niece, etc.)
Yours affectionately
With love
Yours.

Keep these phrases for letters to relatives and close friends. They are impolite when used in official communications or letters to strangers.

1.3.10 Writer's signature and name
The writer's signature and printed name should follow the closing phrase. Do you want your letter answered? Make it easy– print your name below your signature:

Yours sincerely

J H Morgan

Mr James H Morgan

1.3.11 Official title/ position/ office
In business and official letters, it is standard practice to indicate the writer's position in the organisation:

Yours faithfully

M London

Dr Michael London
Medical Director

Titles are helpful to new recruits and outsiders, who would not be able to associate every name with a position or function in the organisation. They are also helpful in future telephone inquiries when somebody may ask, and they often do: *Who is she? What does she do here?*

Role in which you write
Many hospital consultants send out all types of mail under the 'consultant' title even when they are not writing in their capacity as hospital consultants.

Dr John Trainer, a consultant orthopedic surgeon, is chairman of the regional postgraduate surgical training committee. Confusingly he signs letters about regional surgical training matters as:

> Mr. John Trainer MD FRCS
> Consultant Orthopedic Surgeon

Mr. Trainer should 'sign' letters on regional surgical training matters as the chairman of the committee.

> Mr. John Trainer MD FRCS
> Chairman, Regional Surgical Training Committee.

Individuals who perform different roles should make sure the right titles are used to *'sign'* their written communications (letters, e-mails, meno, reports…).

Check. Are you writing as Consultant Physician or as Clinical Director for Medicine?

1.4 Examples of doctors' letters
The following are examples of letters that doctors often write.
- applying for a job
- communicating with a patient (a qualified nurse).

1.4.1 Applying for an SHO post

Dr Indra Shastri
218 Moorside Rd
Urmston
Manchester M41 5SL

Tel. 0161 747 976x
Indra75@hotmail.com

7 September 2003

The Personnel Officer
Bradford Royal Infirmary
Duckworth Lane
Bradford BD9 6RJ

**Re: Application for the post of Senior House Officer in Obstetrics and
Gynaecology** (Ref AOG 357).

I would like to apply the post of Senior House Officer in Obstetrics and Gynaecology
advertised in the BMJ on 31 August 2003.

I have an MD in Obstetrics and Gynaecology from India, have passed PLAB, and
Part 1 of the MRCOG.

After obtaining the MRCOG, I hope to spend 2 years as registrar in reproductive
medicine before returning to work in Kerela, India.

Details of my qualifications, clinical experience, publications and referees are in the
enclosed curriculum vitae.

Yours faithfully
ISShastri
Dr Indra Shastri MB BS MD

2.4.2 Communicating with a patient

Department of Medicine
Whipps Cross Hospital
Whipps Cross Road
Leytonstone
London E17 6EE

22 April 2002

Miss June Matthews
147 Whipps Cross Road
Leytonstone
London E17 6EE

Dear Miss Matthews.

This is to inform you of the results of blood tests from Thursday 4 December 2003. The tests show, as you thought, that you are anaemic (Hb 9.4, MCV 73 and serum ferritin 8).

Your blood has a high level of anti-endomyseal antibody. This strongly suggests you have Coeliac disease– we discussed this possibility in the clinic..

As we discussed, a jejunal biopsy is required to confirm the diagnosis of Coeliac disease before starting a gluten-free diet.

The biopsy could be done as a day procedure on a Monday morning or Wednesday afternoon. Please inform my secretary when in May or June 2003, you prefer to have the biopsy.

Your s sincerely

J Romford

Dr John Romford FRCP

cc. Dr Michael Mandel, 19 Whipps Cross Road, Leytonstone E17 6EE

Summary

- Follow the standard structure for letters
- Give headings or titles to business and official letters
- Quote Reference/ Invoice/ Order/ Customer numbers for fast action
- Write politely; there is no need to document your rudeness
- Give enough details to enable the recipient to respond as required
- Use clear simple words, avoid jargon wherever possible
- Use short words, short sentences, and short paragraphs
- Print your name below your signature in official/business letters.

Further Reading

1. Jarvie G. **Bloomsbury Grammar Guide**. London: Bloomsbury 2000.

2. Strunk W. White EB. **The elements of Style**. London: Longman 1999.

3. Ritter RM. **The Oxford Manual of Style**. Oxford: Oxford University Press 2002.

---

2. Writing a winning CV

Writing a winning CV

2.1 What is a CV?

A CV (curriculum vitae) is a summary of a person's professional life and work (personal details, qualifications, skills and experience, education, work history, other information, hobbies and interests). Curricula vitae (CVs) are called *Career Summaries, Biodata or Resume* in USA.

2.2 Why do you need a CV?

The purpose of a CV is to inform a potential employer of your suitability for the job– to tell them what a good doctor you are. The CV's job is to get you an interview with the employer or his representative.

When you apply for a job, your aim is to convince the recruiter that you are what he/she needs for the job. Like a vendor in an market you display your goods (through your CV or at an interview) to the customer (the recruiter). Your qualifications, skills, experience and personality, [*YOU*], are on sale. In the market the best goods sell first. Similarly the best candidates are selected first (hopefully). Your duty is to present yourself as the best. A good CV is an asset in the competition for jobs, research grants and training positions.

Your CV should be **clear, concise, precise, and simple.** The layout should make it easy for the reader to find information quickly.

You can use your CV to:
• apply for advertised jobs (accompanied by a letter of application)
• inquire about future jobs (accompanied by a letter of inquiry)
• apply for training positions (accompanied by a letter of application)

- apply for research grants (with a proposal and a letter of application)
- provide sorted information when completing application forms.

2.3 Structure of a CV
Medical curricula vitae are as different as the individuals they describe. However they follow a common format.

Usual format for medical CVs.

Short name (***Initials** and **surname** and your major qualification*)
Address:

Telephone (day time):
Fax:
E-mail:

Full Name (*first name(s) followed by SURNAME*)
Date of birth:
Nationality:
Sex:

QUALIFICATIONS
State your qualification(s) dates, institution (college/ university).

PROFESSIONAL ORGANISATIONS
List professional organisations you belong to (may include GMC, BMA, MDU or MPS, royal college, and professional societies and clubs) here.

CAREER PLAN
Briefly state your career plans and how the job will help you achieve them.

EXPERIENCE AND SKILLS
Concisely summarise your main skills and abilities (*essential in a senior*

---

doctor's CV- clinical, managerial/leadership, research, etc).

EDUCATION
Give dates, names of institutions and their location, subjects studied and qualifications gained. Mention outstanding non-academic achievements (leadership roles, prizes and distinctions) here.

WORK HISTORY
Dates, position held, employer's name and location, main duties and achievements.

ADDITIONAL INFORMATION
Useful facts that do not fit well into the above categories may be mentioned here– courses attended, presentations at professional meetings, research, clinical audit and publications (articles and books or chapters in books).

Other useful skills (computer skills, writing, etc) should be mentioned. You can add headings for audits, publications, courses attended, presentations, etc. (*Omit this section if you have no additional information to give*).

INTERESTS (HOBBIES)
Name and briefly describe your hobbies and leisure activities.

REFEREES
Give names, addresses, telephone and fax numbers and e-mail addresses of persons who have agreed to act as your referees– usually two.

The CV should clearly and concisely display personal details, qualification(s), career plans, education, work history, other relevant information (publications, prizes, IT skills, etc) and hobbies.

The order in which the topics appear in the CV will vary slightly depending on individual preferences. However it is best to follow the standard format till you are experienced in writing CVs.

Headings make it easier for the recruiter to find information. If you have worked as a doctor for short time you do not need to worry about writing much on teaching, clinical audit or research. Recruiters do not expect a HO or SHO's CV to contain much on management, clinical governance or publications.

However do include leadership roles you held at school and university, mention research and publications done as a university student, and audits done since graduation.

CVs for senior doctors

Senior doctors create separate sections in their CVs for clinical audit, teaching, research, publications, management and clinical governance. These activities become important with seniority, and are described to show evidence of leadership, drive and achievement.

> *"The CV you used to get your consultant job is unlikely to impress anyone in your new job market. Simply churning out the same CV for every job you go for won't work any more."* Peskett & Empey, BMJ 2003; 327:s179-s180

Senior doctors wishing to take up managerial roles outside clinical medicine must learn to write their CVs to beat the competition from business and the non-clinical side of the NHS.

2.3.1 Personal details

State your postal address, telephone number and e-mail address (if you have one). Give your full names, date of birth, nationality and sex.

Some applicants add hepatitis B status to personal details.

2.3.2 Qualifications

State your qualifications (BSc, MB ChB, MD, etc). Memberships (by examination) of professional bodies (MRCP, MRCS, MRCGP, *etc)* are included in this section. Passes at parts/modules of professional examinations should be listed separately. Do not claim the full qualification after passing part 1! The recruiter will not be impressed.

Failed exams

Some doctors include in their qualifications: *MRCP part 2 (failed)*, or something similar. I do not recommend such a practice. Don't list exams you failed.

If you recently passed part of a membership exam then mention it. Say when you are sitting the next part. If you passed part 1 many years ago, perhaps you should not list it. [*"Shall he ever get the membership? No. Reject."*]

2.3.3 Career plans

Briefly state your future plans and how the job will help you achieve them. Your career plan should be on the first page of the CV. You may have worked in different specialties before finding your niche. Briefly give your reason for applying for the post. Your *Career Plan* should be short and clear. Think about what you intent to achieve before writing the plan. Examples:

- I hope to work in Medicine as an SHO, take the MRCP and specialise in Neurology.

- My intention is to take the MRCS and specialise in Thoracic Surgery

- My plan is to gain the MRCPCH work as a registrar in general and community paediatrics before returning to Botswana.

The recruiter wants to know if the job will help you pass your exams in addition to paying you a living wage. There is no need for long paragraphs, let alone pages of personal statements. So be brief, limit your plan to two lines. A detailed account of your childhood intention to become a surgeon is pedantic.

2.3.4 Experience and skills

A section summarising experience and skills is essential in a senior doctor's CV. HO and SHOs can easily omit it.

Senior doctors should list their main skills and abilities concisely. The aim is to highlight what the employer would get if she employed you. E.g.:

- **teaching–** as an SpR, I supervise and teach medical students and house officers and help senior house officers prepare for the MRCS.

- **leadership–** as clinical director for medicine I supervised the division's transition from an NHS culture into a competitive service provider.

2.3.5 Education

Give dates, names and addresses of institutions you attended, courses taken and examinations passed. Outstanding non-academic achievements should be mentioned (class president, head prefect, athletics captain...) with dates. This is where you can indicate your leadership potential. Example:

1994 - 1999: University of Leeds Medical School (studying for MB ChB)
– secretary Leeds Medical Students Christian Fellowship (1997 - 1998)
– represented university in athletics: 400m and 800m (1996 - 98)

2.3.6 Work history

Give dates, job titles, names of employers and their location, and your duties, and achievements. Employers are interested in what you have done (and can do), and not *empty years of experience.* Example:

July 1998 - June 1999: **Registrar in Paediatrics,** St Johns Hospital, Essex:
– hospital inpatient and outpatient paediatrics and neonatal medicine
– taught clinical skills to medical students and senior house officers
– performed, presented and published two clinical audits (*see Audit*).

Of course you could present these details in full sentences in a continuous paragraph. However prose does not highlight your achievements– they do not stand out. Make it easy for the recruiter to find your skills and achievements. Recent posts are described in detail while those in distant past are outlined.

2.3.7 Research and Publications

If you have done research and published papers cite them. If you have contributed chapters to books or written books, include them here too. Follow the Vancouver style for citing publications and references. Examples:

Citing a paper in a journal:
1. International Committee of Medical Journal Editors. **Uniform Requirements for manuscripts submitted to Biomedical Journals.** *Ann Inter Med* 1997; 126: 36-47.

Citing a published book:
2. **Shorter Oxford English Dictionary**. Oxford: Oxford University Press 2002.

2.3.8 Additional information

This is where you state other information you wish the recruiter to know, but could not easily fit into the other sections:
• general and professional courses you have attended, or are attending
• professional presentations at local and distant meeting and conferences
• special professional, linguistic and technical skills.

2.3.9 Interests/ hobbies

The purpose of this section is to show that you have a life outside medicine. Name and briefly describe your hobbies and leisure activities. If you are a member of a competitive sport team, say so. Your role in the community– charity groups, religious activity or other social group may be described here.

Do not include activities likely to offend prospective employers. Be sensitive in your choice of activities to describe.

2.3.10 Referees

These are people who know you professionally and are able and willing to commend you to a new employer. Ask them if they would be willing to act as your referees.

List the names, addresses, telephone and fax numbers, and e-mail addresses of 2 or 3 people who have *agreed* to comment on your character and professional knowledge and skills. Do not name anybody who has not agreed to be your referee. He/she may not send a reference or worse, send a bad one.

Use people who will put in a good word for you. *If you think a particular person will give you a bad reference do not use her/him as a referee.* Why would you sabotage your application?

2.4 Types of CV

CVs can be written in three slightly different formats– the *Targeted,* the *Chronological* and the *Functional.*

**2.4.1 A *targeted CV* **names the target job, states capabilities (skills) and summarises the candidate's work experience. It:
- gives personal details (names, date of birth, sex, etc)
- lists academic qualifications and other accomplishments
- names the target position (the job he/she is looking for)
- gives his work experience at school, college and later
- names and briefly describes hobbies and other interests, and
- gives names, and contact details of referees.

A targeted CV is suitable for a young candidate who is looking for his first substantive job. It is ideal for non-professional graduates entering public services or business. A targeted CV works well for the HO and SHO, but is rarely adequate for more senior doctors.

**2.4.2 A *chronological CV* **gives personal details and qualifications and lists work experience chronologically (from the first job to the last or most recent). Chronological CVs are suitable for candidates who want to stay in the same industry or profession, who have relatively short work records or have not changed jobs frequently. Some doctors prefer chronological CVs and if well crafted, convey essential information adequately.

2.4.3 A functional CV lists personal details and professional qualifications, *highlights functional competencies* (skills and experience) and summarises work history from current or most recent position back to the first.

By the time most doctors become registrars (let alone GPs principals or consultants) they have changed jobs and job titles many times. A chronological CV would not display their skills and experience to their advantage. A functional CV is required to do their careers justice.

As responsibilities and achievements increase from house officer through registrar to consultant or GP principal, so does the length and complexity of the CV. Functional CVs are ideal for presenting the details most senior doctors want to include in their CVs.

Because doctors change jobs frequently, it is tedious if the same details are listed under every post. With the passage of time (experience) it becomes desirable to highlight essential skills and experience to reduce the tedium of repeating identical job descriptions.

Functional CVs are appropriate for senior doctors– registrars looking for consultant jobs or consultants and GP principals changing employers or moving into management.

2.5 Crafting the CV

Many young doctors, particularly those who trained abroad, are afraid of writing their CVs. They fear that they will get it wrong. Like all activities, performance improves with good practice. You are an expert at walking, talking, reading and writing. But how many times did you fall onto your bottom before you could walk steadily? Just as you learnt to walk, talk and write, with many mistakes, so will you learn to write CVs– practice!

Initially you will make a few mistakes, but you will master the skill soon.

Writing CVs is a skill that every worker whose livelihood depends on securing appointments through open competition must learn. It is essential to marketing your professional skills– to finding new and may be better jobs. So find time, patience and the will to learn the skill.

2.5.1 Confusion about writing and typing

Some doctors confuse **typing** a CV with **writing** one. By writing, I mean selecting and putting the information in a particular order to produce an informative summary of your professional life and work (personal details, qualifications, clinical experience, education and other interests). That summary can then be typed and printed to produce a CV.

When a recruiter starts reading your CV you probably have less than a minute or two to convince her/him of your suitability for the job. A good first impression is vital. Your CV must present your personal and professional attributes to meet the requirements of the post.

2.5.2 Composing a CV

Composing a good CV takes time and effort. However, given that the average doctor changes jobs at least three times within two years of graduation, that he/she will reply to 5 to 30 or more adverts before getting a job position, any effort spent on composing a CV is a wise investment– paying off in invitations for interview.

Unfortunately internet CV examples are not suitable for medical positions. They are *targeted* at people seeking jobs in the private sector (business mainly). Medical recruiters expect more detailed documents.

To prepare your CV, use *'Usual format for medical CVs'* to make notes, type

Writing the medical CV

the notes and rearrange them into a document whose *'look'* resembles one of the examples in section 2.12 (junior doctors), and 2.13 (senior doctors), below.

2.6 Quality of CV

Your CV should have a neat, attractive layout. It should be printed on good quality white paper with a good printer (inkjet or laser are best). If you do not know how to type, you should learn. Buy typing/keyboard skills software and teach yourself on your computer. If you use a typewriter you should get a new black ribbon. Better still pay a qualified secretary to type your CV.

Quality and weight (thickness) of paper

Hospitals, universities and business use $80gm/m^2$ paper for their documents. Yet some applicants for SHO jobs print their CVs on thick expensive paper. Recruiters are not impressed by the thickness or cost of the paper, but by what is written on it. There are many varieties of good white $80gm/m^2$ printing paper on the market. It is not necessary to use paper heavier than $100gm/m^2$ for a CV.

2.7 Language of your CV

Mind your grammar and spelling. Use a spellchecker or a dictionary, and **then read the document carefully.** The spellchecker does not distinguish between *hear* and here, *were* and *wear*, *their* and there, and many other words with similar sounds but different spelling and meaning.

Poor spelling and bad grammar whisper to the recruiter.....
"I do not have an English dictionary"
"I can't bother to use a spellchecker"
"Do not trust me to do anything right"
"I am not interested in the job."

Bad spelling and poor grammar invite the recruiter to *'reject' your application.* Your CV should be written in an active language. Emphasise your achievements, skills, and contributions to teams you have worked with.

Use action words wherever possible. They give the impression of an active,
decisive individual. Examples:

achieved	co-ordinated	organised	sampled	
advised	examined	organised	taught	
audited	managed	performed	tested	etc.

- performed, presented and published two clinical audits (*see Audits*)
- advised Catsford Community Health Council on clinical governance
- established a district diabetes team of physicians, nurses and dieticians
- taught emergency medicine to medical students and house officers.

2.8 Length of CV

Academic and medical institutions insist on detailed CVs with every job and
publication listed. Your CV should give enough details to convey your skills and
experience adequately. Its length will depend on the number of jobs you have
held, clinical audits, research and publications, presentations and courses you
have attended. Two pages should suffice for a PRHO seeking his first SHO
post; while a registrar applying for a consultant post may need several pages.

However a consultant or principal GP looking for a managerial job must write a
short, focused CV– may be two or three pages long– to summarise his skills
and achievements. The traditional medical CV will not impress human resource
directors, no chief executives of government quangos.

2.9 What to leave out of your CV

Your CV should present you in the best light. On its strength you will either be
selected for interview or rejected. You have control of the quality of your CV.

No lies or fabrications in CVs

Emphasise your achievements. Do not portray yourself in a negative way; but your CV should be based on the truth. Lies must be purged from the CV:

> **The GMC Professional Conduct Committee found a doctor guilty of serious professional misconduct after she made false claims about her academic achievements and employment history. The Committee suspended her registration for 12 months** (GMC News 14 October 2002)

Dr Chieke did not mention that she retook Surgery exams at university. Neither did she apologise for her poor netball skills. She enjoys ballroom dancing and Igbo music and is happy to talk about either at interview.

In **Managing interviews,** we shall discuss how to talk about past failures– as learning experiences!

2.10 Commercial CV writers

Several companies **produce** CVs. However you should not assume that they will **write** a CV for you. They do not know about your education, qualifications, leadership skills, clinical experience, no about your hobbies and interests. You will still have to write these out before the company can *type and print* (**produce**) the CV.

Commercial CV writers help with layout and editing but **only you can write your CV**. They charge a premium (a lot of money) for editing your writing (cutting out unnecessary or irrelevant detail) and for typing and printing the result. They print the CV on unnecessarily expensive paper and charge you for the privilege!

Do not waste good money paying a private company to produce a CV for you. Sorry, if you want a winning CV, you must create it yourself. Write and then edit it and **pay for typing and printing.** It is cheaper that way.

2.11 Keep your CV up to-date

Update your CV each time there is a significant change in your career or you achieve something important (change jobs, complete and present an audit, publish a paper or take on new clinical or leadership duties).

When required, rewriting the CV will be easy. All the information will be there waiting to be arranged according to the needs of the new post.

Many capable applicants have missed good positions because their CVs were untidy or plainly irrelevant. Does your CV convey your skills and capabilities, work record and achievements concisely and clearly? Revise it till it does.

2.12 CVs for junior doctors

The following examples should demonstrate how a CV is crafted from an individual's personal attributes and professional history.

The CV examples anticipate important questions:
- Who is he (age, sex, nationality)?
- What does she expect to gain from this job?
- What are her qualifications/skills and experience?
- Is he/she likely to be an asset to our department?

1. Dr Smyth (*page 41*) wants an SHO post in Surgery
2. Dr Sandhu (*page 44*) seeks an SHO post in Paediatrics
3. Dr Chieke (*page 48*) hopes for an SpR post in Medicine.

Only Dr Smyth names referees in his CV. The others plan to name them in the cover letter and so are free to use different people without changing their CVs.

Dr RH Smyth MB ChB

Address: 231 Seymour Grove
               Old Trafford
               Manchester M16 0LW

Telephone: 0161 564 769x
               077 5416 861x
               email: rhsmyth@hotmail.com

Name: **Richard Henry SMYTH**
Date of Birth: 15 March 1976
Gender: Male
Nationality   British
Hepatitis B Immune

QUALIFICATIONS
MB ChB 1998, University of Leeds, Leeds, UK

Passed MRCS part 1 in April 2003.

CAREER INTENTION
I hope to complete the MRCS exams in 2005, and specialise in orthopaedics

PROFESSIONAL ORGANISATIONS
Fully registered with the General Medical Council
Member of the British Medical Association
Member of the Medical Protection Society

EDUCATION

1993 -1998: University of Leeds Medical School (MB ChB studies)
– secretary Leeds Medical Students Christian Fellowship (1997-1998)
– represented university in athletics (400m and 800m, and 400m relay)
– captain university athletics team at UK universities championships (1999)

CURRENT APPOINTMENT

*Aug 2002- to date: **Senior house officer in Surgery**,* Royal Bolton Hospital:
– member of BMA junior doctors committee (2002- to-date).
– audited "Drug details in discharge letters for patients with duodenal ulcers"

PAST APPOINTMENTS

*Aug 1999 - Aug 2000: **Senior House Officer, Emergency Medicine**,*
Catsford Infirmary, Catsford:
– president Junior Doctors Mess (2000)
– audited "missed non-accidental injuries in infants' fractures" June 2000.

Aug 1998 - Aug 1999: ***House Officer**,* Royal Bolton Hospital, Bolton
– house officer in Surgery (6 months) and General Medicine (6months)
– entertainment secretary, Junior Doctors Mess (1999)

AUDIT

1. *June 2000: **Missed non-accidental fractures in infant's**,* Catsford
Infirmary. With a senior SpR in radiology, I reviewed X-rays of the humerus
in infants seen in with painful, swollen arms over 12 months. Four spiral
fractures and corresponding hospital records were found. Only three were
invested for non-accidental injury.

2. *Nov 2002: "**Discharge rug details patients with duodenal ulcers**"*
Royal Bolton Hospital. Discharge letters of 25 patient s with H. pylori IgG
were analysed. Drug names, doses and length of therapy were no given in
19; drug names were only found in 4; in 2 "home on antibiotics" was found.

COURSES ATTENDED
1. *Basic Surgical Life Support*, Bolton, March 1999
2. **Advanced Surgical Life Support**, Manchester, Nov. 1999.
3. **Basic Sciences for MRCS**, Manchester, Dec. 2000

COMPUTER SKILLS
• Skilled in using Microsoft Word, Excel and Power Point
• Competent in internet literature searches with Medline and PUBMED.

HOBBIES
Amateur athletics, Football
Medical politics

REFEREES

Dr M Karim FRCP	**Mr James Forte** FRCS
Consultant Physician	Consultant in Emergency Medicine
Royal Bolton Hospital	Catsford Infirmary,
Minerva Rd	Lloyd George Avenue
Bolton. BL4 OJR	Catsford CZ65 4GH
Tel: 01204 390758.	Te. 011x 34562x
Fax: 01204 390x34	Fax: 011x 34562x
mkarim@hotmail.com	james.forte@forte.co.uk

Dr N Sandhu MB BS MD

Address: 59 Gordon Villa
Infirmary Road
Blackburn BB2 3LP

Telephone: 077912367x6 (mobile)
E-mail: nsandhu@hotmail.com

Name: **Nishan SANDHU**
Nationality: Indian
Date of birth: 9th April 1973
Sex: Male

Hepatitis B Immune

QUALIFICATIONS

MB BS, August 1998, University of Delhi, New Delhi, India
MD (Paediatrics), August 2001, University of Delhi, New Delhi, India

Passed PLAB January 20003; eligible for limited registration.
Passed Part 1 MRCPCH, September 2003.

CAREER INTENTION

I hope to work in Paediatrics, take the MRCPCH and specialise in General Paediatrics with an interest in Neonatal Medicine.

PROFFESIONAL ORGANISATIONS
Eligible for Limited registration with GMC, No: 6047x63
Registered with Medical Council of India

SKILLS AND EXPERIENCE
Paediatrics and neonatal medicine
– have managed common paediatric emergencies, investigated and
   performed therapeutic procedures on wards and in emergency rooms
– managed well newborns and neonates in intensive care.

Teaching skills
– taught medical students, interns, senior house officers and nurse students
–instructed in Neonatal Advanced Life Support in Safdarjang Hospital.

Leadership skills
–secretary, then president of Delhi Medical Students Union (1995-6)
– organised 10 neonatal resuscitation workshops for health professionals
– organised and choreographed university fashion show (1994).

EDUCATION
July 1992 – Dec 1997: College of Medical Sciences, University of Delhi
and Guru Teg Bhadur Teaching Hospital; awarded MB BS in August 1998:
–secretary, then president of Delhi Medical Students Union (1995-6)
– organised and choreographed university fashion shows (1995).
– internship in surgery, medicine, obstetrics and gynaecology, preventive
   medicine and paediatrics)

*May1998 – May 2001: **Postgraduate Trainee in Paediatrics,*** Vardhman
Mahavir Medical College, New Delhi (MD Paediatrics)
– MD thesis on *"Effect of intravenous set replacement on neonatal sepsis".*

CLINICAL ATTACHMENT

13 Jan – 14 March 2003: **Clinical Attachment in Paediatrics**, Catsford Infirmary, Catsford.

WORK EXPERINCE

June 2001 - Nov 2002: **Senior Resident (Registrar) in Paediatrics,** Safdarjang Hospital, New Delhi
– 2nd on call for general paediatrics and neonatal intensive care
– worked in asthma, haematology and neonatal follow-up clinic
– taught medical students, interns and senior house officers.
– instructor in neonatal resuscitation to nurses and junior doctors

May1998 – May 2001: **Postgraduate Trainee in Paediatrics,** Safdarjang Hospital, New Delhi
– general paediatrics (18 months), neonatal intensive care (6 months)
  haematology (6 months), cardiology and nephrology (3 month each)
– attended course in neonatal life support and qualified as an instructor
– instructor in neonatal resuscitation to nurses and junior doctors.

July 1996 – Dec 1997: **training intern,** Guru Teg Bhadur Teaching Hospital:
– rotation through surgery, medicine, obstetrics and gynaecology, medicine
  paediatrics preventive
– president of Delhi Medical Students Union (1995-6)

RESEARCH

2001: **Effect of Intravenous set replacement on neonatal sepsis.**
A thesis based on the study was accepted for the MD in Paediatrics, Delhi University.

PUBLICATION

1. Sandhu N, et al. **"Amelia" (congenital absence of limbs).** Case report. Accepted for publication by *Indian Paediatrics,* September 2002.

2. Sandhu N, et al. **Microbiology of IV catheters neonatal sepsis.** *Delhi Medical Journal* 2001; 92(6): 210-212.

PRESENTATIONS

1. Oct. 2000: *Effect of Intravenous set replacement on neonatal sepsis;* 11th Congress, Federation of Asia and Oceania Perinatal Societies, Manila.

2. Nov 2000: *Microbiology of IV catheters neonatal sepsis.* 20th Annual Convention of National Neonatology Forum, Mumbai, India.

COURSES ATTENDED

1. *Nov. 2000: Paediatric Advanced Life Support.* Ganga Ram Hospital, Delhi.

2. *Sept. 2000: Advanced Paediatric and Neonatal Intensive Care.* New Delhi

3. 3 Feb 2002: *Neonatal Ventilation,* All India Institute Medical Sciences. New Delhi

CONFERENCES ATTENDED

1. *Nov. 2000:* International Child Neurology Education., New Delhi.

2. *Dec. 2000:* Current Perspectives in Paediatrics, New Delhi.

3. *May 2001*: International Conference on Paediatric Cardiology, New Delhi.

ADDITIONAL INFORMATION
IT Skills– skilled in using MSWord, Power-point and Internet
Charity work– Child Relief and You (CRY) for helping poor children in India.

HOBBIES
Travelling, Dance and Drama.

Dr E. Chieke MRCP

Address: 14 Campion Close
             Eccleshall
             Stafford ST21 6SR

Telephone   077 374x44 (mobile)
e-mail: echieke@yahoo.co.uk

Name: **Ebele CHIEKE**
Nationality: Nigerian
Date of birth: 16th June 1969
Sex: Female

PROFESSIONAL QUALIFICATIONS
MB ChB, December 1992, University of Benin, Nigeria
MRCP, July 2001, Royal Colleges of Physicians, UK

PROFESSIONAL BODIES
Full Registration with the GMC
Member of the Medical Defence Union
Member of the Royal Colleges of Physicians of London.

CAREER INTENTION
I would like to specialise in Medicine and obtain the CCST in General
Medicine with an interest in Infectious Diseases.

ˊSKILLS AND EXPERIENCE

General medicine
– skilled in diagnosing and managing common tropical diseases
– competent in geriatrics and general medicine (in particular endocrinology, cardiology, nephrology, respiratory and gastroenterology).

Teaching
– teach medical students, and senior house officers using traditional and problem based learning methods
– organise practical sessions in clinical methods for MRCP candidates
– present cases at hospital medical clinico-pathological meetings.

Clinical audit
– performed, presented several audits; two were published (*see Audit*).
– help senior house officers with clinical audit projects.

Management/leadership skills:
– served as Secretary of Benin University Students Union (1991- 92),
– co-ordinate senior house officers' duty rotas and teaching sessions
– serve on Medical Directorate Clinical Effective Committee (2002).

EDUCATION
1987 -1992: University of Benin, Benin, Nigeria (for the MB ChB)
– distinctions in Pathology, Biochemistry, Medicine and Public Health
– secretary of Benin Medical Students Association (1991- 92),

CURRENT APPOINTMENT
Aug.2001- to date: **LAT in Infectious Diseases,** Catsford Infirmary, Catsford:
– inpatient and outpatient management of infectious conditions

– middle grade cover for general medicine and care of the elderly
– teach medical students house officers, and senior house officers.

PREVIOUS APPOINTMENTS

Aug 2000 - July 2001: **Senior house officer in Medicine**, Leeds Infirmary
– inpatient and outpatient management of general medical conditions
– taught medical students and house officers.

Jan 1999 - July 2000: Preparing for and taking PLAB exams, and doing an
8-week clinical attachment in General Medicine in Bradford Royal Infirmary.

Sept 1996 - Dec 1998: **Registrar in Medicine,** Benin University Hospital:
– hospital inpatient and ambulatory general medicine practice
– taught and supervised medical students and house officers
– president, junior doctors' mess (1997).

Jan 1994- Aug 1996: **Medical officer** in the Nigerian Army
– compulsory national service; provided medical care in rural army posts.
– taught and supervised medical auxiliaries.

Jan - Dec 1993: **Pre-registration house officer**, Benin University Hospital.
– 3 months in Paediatrics, Obstetrics/gynaecology, Medicine and Surgery.

RESEARCH

Ischaemic heart disease and income. Benin University Hospital (1997*).*
Ischaemic heart disease and myocardial infarction were commoner in
affluent males, and less among poor males and in females.

AUDIT

Documentation of erythromycin therapy in mycoplasma pneumonia.
Catsford Infirmary, June 2002. 100 discharge letters of patients treated for mycoplasma pneumonia (over 3 years) were analysed. 75 named the drug (erythromycin), the dosage and duration of therapy; 20 named the drug only, and in 8 only "antibiotic given" was found.

A paper based on the audit has been submitted to *Journal of Clinical Audit.*

PUBLICATION

Chieke E, et. al. **Ischaemic heart disease and male income**. *Benin Medical Journal 1998;* 3(4):34-36.

PRESENTATIONS

1. *Sept 1997:*. **Ischaemic heart disease and income in male.** Annual Meeting of Nigeria Cardiological Association, Abuja, Nigeria.

2. *Nov 2001:* **Documentation of erythromycin therapy in mycoplasma pneumonia.** Quarterly Audit Meeting, Catsford Infirmary, Catsford.

COURSES ATTENDED

1. *May 1995:* **Prevention of sexual transmitted disease in soldiers.** Lagos, Nigeria.

2. *March. 1996:* **Management of pulmonary tuberculosis.** University of Lagos, Nigeria.

3. *June 2001:* **Cardiology for the MRCP.** Wythenshawe Hospital, Manchester.

4. *Dec 2001:* **Advanced Medical Life Support**. Catsford Infirmary, Catsford

5. *March 2002:* **Managing HIV infection in pregnancy**. Catsford Infirmary.

HOBBIES
Ballroom dancing
Listening to Igbo music.

2.13 CVs for senior doctors

CVs for senior doctors should be short despite the long service. They should contain information on clinical, and leadership skills roles. Some senior doctors may be full-time clinicians, others clinician-managers while a few are in full time management.

> *The CV you used to get your consultant job is unlikely to impress anyone in your new job market. Simply churning out the same CV for every job you go for won't work any more.* Peskett & Empey, BMJ 2003; 327:s179-s180

Senior doctors should therefore emphasise different aspects of their experience and achievements in response to the desired post's person specifications. They must pick and mix relevant skills and achievements to create CVs that answers the recruiter's needs.

Clinicians moving into management

A senior doctor aspiring to full time management should write his CV to fit the expectations of human resource directors and chief executives of organisations he/she wishes to join. Unlike hospitals, these chiefs prefer short focused documents that highlight skills and achievements– in 2 pages or so. Non-medic applicants– the competition– will submit 2 page focused CVs; so should you.

The following are fictitious examples of CVs sent by senior doctors:
- Dr A Walker is searching for a consultant post (*page 53*)
- Dr M Khan, a locum consultant, wants substantive post (*page 62*)
- Mr S Chester has updated his CV– might apply for divisional directorship
- Dr S Murray hopes to become medical director of a quango (*page 69*).

Dr AP Walker MSc MRCP

Address: 112 Park Rd
            Timperley
            Altrincham WA14 5AB

Telephone: 077912367x6 (mobile)
            0161 6x2 9345 (evenings)
E-mail: apwalker@hotmail.com

Name: **Dr Adam Peter WALKER**
Date of birth: 01 October 1967
Nationality: British
Sex: Male

QUALIFICATIONS
MB ChB   1992, University of Southampton
MSc   1996 community child health, University of Keele
MRCP(UK) 1997 Royal Colleges of Physicians of UK

CAREER PLAN
I have completed specialist training in hospital and community paediatrics.
I am looking for consultant post that combines hospital paediatrics and
community child health.

SKILLS AND EXPERIENCE

- ***Neonatal and general paediatrics*** skills and knowledge from 10 years of paediatric practice (8 years at registrar level).

- ***Community child health skills***
  - one year MSc course with clinical work in community child health
  - a year of formal SpR training that emphasised developmental paediatrics and special educational needs, child health surveillance, child protection, behavioural issues and child psychiatry, and childhood physical disability.

- ***Leadership and management***
  - organise OSCE paediatric clinical case for medical student exams
  - trainee representative to regional paediatric training committee
  - attended *"creating effective leaders"* course at Leeds Business School.

- ***Clinical governance***
  - contribute to effective patient safety and clinical risk management
  - served on paediatrics clinical governance committee in Oldham.

- ***Teaching***
  - organise 'cases' for 4th year medical student OSCE exams
  - organise teaching programmes for senior house officers
  - teach junior doctors preparing for the MRCPCH examinations.

- ***Clinical audit and research***
  - I supervise senior house officers in clinical audit and audit report writing
  - have performed and presented several audits (see *Audit*).
  - have researched and published articles (*see Research*).

CURRENT EMPLOYMENT

04 Mar 2002 – to date: **Specialist Registrar (SpR) in Neonatology,** Hope Hospital, Salford:
– normal baby care, neonatal intensive care, neonatal and paediatric on call
– bay transport (resuscitation, stabilisation and retrieval of sick neonates)
– organise educational meetings for senior house officers and nurses
– participate in clinical governance and risk management meetings.

PREVIOUS EMPLOYMENT

04 Feb – 01 Mar 02: **Locum Consultant Paediatrician,** Catsford Infirmary:
– general paediatric and neonatal medicine with on call duties
– general paediatrics, neurology and neuro-disability clinics
– taught and supervised junior paediatricians.

01 Mar 01 – 28 Feb 02: **SpR Community Paediatrics,** Salford NHS Trust:
– on call for general paediatrics and neonates medicine
– baby clinics: immunisation, nutrition, growth and behaviour advice
– *developmental assessment*: learnt and performed Griffith assessments
– *child protection*: examined suspected child abuse cases, wrote reports, attended case conferences and gave evidence in court
– neuro-disability and special educational needs clinics and administration
– *child psychiatry*: assessing for ADHD, and autism and behaviour problem
– *audiology*: learned role of audiometry and tympanometry in hearing loss
– examined 'looked after' children and attended adoption panels.

Sep 2000 – Feb 2001: **SpR in Paediatrics,** St Mary's Hospital, Manchester:
– general paediatric and neurology clinics
– on call for general paediatrics and neonatology
– neonatal transport (resuscitation, stabilisation and retrieval)
– taught and supervised senior house officers.

*Mar 2000 - Aug 2000: **SpR in Clinical Genetics,** Royal Manchester
Children's Hospital, Manchester:*
– dysmorphology, neuromuscular, ophthalmological and cancer clinics
– on call for paediatric intensive care and neonates at Hope Hospital.

*01 Sep 1999 – 29 Feb 2000: **SpR in Respiratory Medicine,***
Royal Manchester Children's Hospital (RMCH), Manchester:
– cystic fibrosis clinics, worked with liaison nurse helping families
– learnt to perform and interpret lung function tests; recognise and manage
  bronchiectasis, tuberculosis and other respiratory diseases.

*Mar 1999 – Aug 1999: **SpR in Paediatric Oncology,** RMCH, Manchester:*
– worked in haematology and solid tumours clinics; on call for oncology.
– contributed to the care of bone marrow transplant children
– prepared haematology slides and learnt to interpret bone marrows exams.

*Sep 1998 – Feb 1999: **SpR in Paediatric Intensive Care,** RMCH:*
– learnt to manage critically sick children and counsel their relatives
– advised referring hospitals on stabilisation before transfer
– retrieved sick children for paediatric intensive care.

*Sep 1997- Aug 1998: **SpR in Paediatrics,** Wythenshawe Hospital,
Manchester*
– general paediatric and neonatal practice; on call for both
– worked in neurology, nephrology, cardiology, cystic fibrosis and allergy
– taught and supervised senior house officers and medical students
– served as lead doctor for BCG immunisation in the neonatal unit.

*Sep 96 – Aug 97: **SpR in Paediatrics,** Royal Bolton Hospital, Bolton*
– worked in general paediatrics and neonatal medicine; on call for both
– gained experience in child health surveillance and immunisation

Sept 95 – Aug 96: **MSc in community child health,** University of Keele.
– attached to, and worked with Solihull community child health team
– attended modular course in Keele, took exams and wrote a dissertation
– MSc dissertation "*Immunisation uptake among children in foster care.*"

Aug 94 – Aug 95: **Senior House Officer (SHO) in Paediatrics** Birmingham Heartlands Hospital, Birmingham:
– neonatal intensive care (6 months) general paediatrics (6 months).

Aug 93 - Jul 94: **SHO in Paediatrics,** Canterbury Hospital, Kent
– neonatal and paediatric experience; on call for both
– child health surveillance and immunisation sessions

Aug 92- Jul 93: **House Officer,** Southampton General Hospital (Surgery and them Medicine)

CLINICAL AUDIT
1. Follow up of children admitted with acute gastro-enteritis and whose stool contained pathogens, Hope Hospital, Kent, May 1994:

Target– All children discharged after resolution of acute diarrhoea should receive at least one home visit from the community nursing team.

Cases notes of 26 of 35 children admitted with acute gastro-enteritis in March to August 1993 were analysed. Stool samples from 9 children had pathogens. Community nurses visited 4 at least once.

I recommended that a named community nurse should follow children discharged after acute diarrhoea. This should be re-audited in a year.

2. BCG uptake by babies admitted to neonatal unit, Wythenshawe Hospital, Manchester, June 1998 (A re-audit):
Target– All babies at risk of tuberculosis should receive BCG immunisation

Case notes of eligible neonates (Feb to Aug 1997) were examined for a record of BCG immunisation. A previous audit found a 32% BCG immunisation rate.

Of 32 qualifying records studied, 24 (67%) had a record of BCG immunisation, 6 were not immunised for lack of consent or early discharge. In two cases it was not possible to decide if BCG was given or not. I recommended that a senior nurse should be responsibility for ensuring BCG immunisation.

3. RSV status in babies with bronchiolitis admitted for intensive care. RMCH, Manchester January 2000:
Target– RSV status of children treated for bronchiolitis should be documented. Case notes of 45 admissions for bronchiolitis (Nov – Feb 1999) were scrutinised. A record of nasopaharyngeal aspirates for RSV at the referring hospital or in the unit was found in 27 (60%).

I recommended that RSV status of bronchiolitic babies should be sought and recorded in case notes. A re-audit was suggested for the 2000 winter cases.

RESEARCH
1. Immunisation uptake among children in foster care. Solihull, Feb-April 1996. Immunisation records of children age 16 months to 5 years in foster care were scrutinised for completeness of immunisations.

Most of the delay in completing immunisations occurred before children went into foster care. When informed, most foster parents presented children for catch up doses. 40% of fostered children were not fully immunised because social workers and child health staff did not know that some children were not fully immunised, or did not inform foster parents in get them immunised.

2. *Medical contribution to child protection investigations in Salford and Trafford,* January 2002. I examined the adequacy of child protection medical reports in Salford and Trafford NHS Trusts between January 2000 and December 2001

Social service records in Trafford and Salford falling under Section 47 of the 1989 Children's Act, were sampled. 50 records from each trust were scrutinised against a list of items a child protection medical report should cover.

9 of 18 medical assessment in Trafford were done by general practitioners, while all 6 in Salford were done by paediatricians. Ten (55.5%) reports from Trafford and 5 (83%) from Salford contained all essential items.

PUBLICATIONS
1. Walker AP. *Immunisation uptake among children in foster care.* *J Community Paediatrics* 1997; 5(3):23-25.
2. *Walker AP, James D.* **Parent *recall of information given at diagnosis of meningitis in their children.*** *Journal of Patient Opinion* 2002; 2(3): 34-35.

COURSES ATTENDED
1. Sept 1998: ***Management strategies in Paediatric Intensive Care.*** Bristol.

2. Sept 1999. ***Health Service Management.*** David Allen Centre, Manchester

3. Dec 2000. *Creating Effective Leaders Training.* Cumbria.

4. Sept 2001. *Advance Paediatric Life Support .* Manchester.

5. July 2001. *Griffith Developmental Assessment.* Trafford, Manchester.

6. May 2002. *Foundation Course in Child Protection.* Pendelbury, Salford.

7. Dec 2002. *Update on infectious diseases.* St Mary's Hospital, London.

PRESENTATIONS

1. April 1997: **Immunisation uptake among children in foster care.**
Annual Royal College of Paediatric and Child Health, York.

2. *Oct 1999.* **BCG uptake by babies admitted to neonatal unit at**
Wythenshawe Hospital. Annual National Audit Meeting, Edinburgh,

3. *Oct 2001.* **Medical contribution to child protection investigations in**
Salford NHS Trust. North West British Association of Community Child
Health Meeting, Clitheroe, Lancashire.

HOBBIES
Country side walking
Medical history.

Writing the medical CV

Dr M A Khan FRCPCH

Address	11 Whittington Mews
	London N12 8QF

Telephone/fax:	0208 343 829X0
	Mobile: 07952 7451X7
	makhan54@hotmai.com

Name	**Mohamed Asif KHAN**
Date of Birth	9 June 1954
Sex	Male
Marital Status	Married
Nationality	British

Hepatitis B Immune

QUALIFICATIONS

BSc 1977, Multan University, Pakistan
MB BS 1980, Punjab University, Lahore, Pakistan
MRCP(UK) 1988, (Paediatrics) Royal Colleges of Physicians, UK
FRCPCH 1997, Royal College of Paediatrics and Child Health, UK

CAREER PLAN

I am looking forward to working as a consultant paediatrician and lead clinician for diabetes.

PROFESSIONAL ORGANISATIONS

Full GMC Registration and as a Specialist in Paediatrics

Member, Royal Colleges of Physicians, UK

Fellow, Royal College of Paediatrics and Child Health

Member, Medical Defence Union

SKILLS AND EXPERIENCE

General paediatrics and neonatology

– have wide experience in general paediatrician and neonatal medicine

– have developed an interest in Diabetes and hold a Certificate in Diabetes

Leadership and management

– served as clinical director for a multinational team of paediatricians

– chaired Hospital Continuous Medical Education Committee

Clinical audit

– represented paediatrics on the Hospital Clinical Audit Support Group

– supervised junior doctors in several clinical audits in paediatrics

Clinical governance

– attuned to clinical governance and risk management issues

– promote clinical governance through training to enhance clinical
   competence, clinical guidelines and clinical audit.

Teaching

– taught clinical paediatrics to medical students and residents

– taught paediatric residents for Arab Board in Paediatric (1992-2002)

– teach senior house officers and registrars in current post in NHS

Research

I have done several clinical studies that lead to publications:

– Impact of an antimicrobial policy in an Arabian hospital (1998)

– Clinical features and investigations in urinary tract infection (1994)

APPOINTMENTS

Sept 2002 – to date: **Locum Consultant Paediatrician**, Catsford Infirmary:
–general paediatrics work, and contributed to consultant of the week rota.

– teach medical students, senior house officers and registrars in paediatrics

Nov 2000 - Aug 02: **Consultant Paediatrician,** Armed Forces Hospital Khamis Mushayt, Kingdom of Saudi Arabia (KSA):

– hospital and ambulatory general paediatric and neonatal medicine

– lead paediatrician in paediatric diabetes and nephrology

– established a regional diabetic service with trained nurses and dieticians

– deputy clinical director of a multinational paediatric team and support staff

– teacher and examiner in paediatrics for King Khaled University

– taught junior doctors taking the MRCPCH and Arab Board exams

Jan 1994 - Nov 2000: **Consultant Paediatrician**, King Khalid Hospital, Hail, KSA

– hospital general paediatrics and neonatal medicine practice

– clinical director of a multinational team of paediatricians (1996-2000)

– served as chairman Continuous Medical Education Committee

– developed ambulatory paediatric service to serve distant communities

– taught residents for the MRCPCH and Arab Board exams in Paediatrics.

Dec 1992 - Dec. 93: **Consultant Paediatrician**, Rafiq Hospital, Qatif, KSA:

– general paediatric and neonatal medicine and diabetes care

– gained skill *sickle cell diseases, G6PD deficiency, thalassemia and inborn errors of metabolism (causes of* 20% clinic work and admissions)
– taught paediatrics to medical students and junior paediatricians

1988 - Nov. 92: **Lecture in Paediatrics**, Karachi Medical Institute, Pakistan:
– general paediatric and neonatal medicine and diabetes clinic work
– taught paediatrics to medical students and junior paediatricians
– helped junior doctors prepare for postgraduate exams in paediatrics

*Jul. 1987 - Jul. 88: **Registrar in Paediatrics***, St Luke's Hospital, Bradford
– neonatal medicine (6 months) and general paediatrics (6 months)
– leant to perform neonatal cranial ultrasound scans and jejunal biopsies.

*Jul. 1986 - Jul 87: **Senior SHO in Paediatrics***, Leighton Hospital, Crewe.
*Dec. 1985 - Jun 86: **Senior SHO in Paediatrics***, Park Hospital, Urmston.

Jun. 1984 – Dec 85: **SHO in Paediatrics**, Basildon Hospital, Basildon.

*Jul. 1983 - May 84: **Locum SHO in Paediatrics***, Various NHS hospitals

June. 1981 - Feb 83: **Senior House Officer in Paediatrics,** Nishtar Hospital, Multan, Pakistan

Jun. 1980 – May 1981: **House Officer**, Nishtar Hospital, Multan, Pakistan (6 months in Medicine and 6 months in Surgery).

PUBLICATIONS
1. Khan MA, et al. ***Impact of an antimicrobial policy in an Arabian hospital*** (1998) *Saudi Pharm J* 1998; 6(1): 74-79

2. Khan MA, et al, *Neonatal Systemic Candidiasis in Al-Rafiq Hospital.* *Saudi Med J* 1995; 16: 556-560

3. Khan MA. *Iron deficiency anaemia.* The Practitioner 1995; 6(11):781 (East Mediterranean Edition)

4. Khan MA, et al. **Clinical features and investigations in urinary tract infection.** *Specialist Pak J Med Sci* 1994; 10(3):209-213

5. Khan MA. *Systemic lupus erythematosis.* The Practitioner 1994, 5(1):7 (East Mediterranean Edition);

6. Khan MA. *Clinical, laboratory features of urinary tract infection* (1994) *Specialist Pak J Med Sci,* 1992; 8(4):63-66

COURSES AND SYMPOSIA ATTENDED

1. *25-26 Nov 2003: Child Protection Training for Senior Doctors.* South Staffordshire NHS Trust

2. *17-18 Nov 2003: Neonatal & Paediatric Ventilation Course.* Institute of Child Health, London.

3. *Oct 2003: Mastering Clinical Audit* (DLC), University of Edinburgh

4. 16 July 2003: *Communication Skills for Consultants.* Frimley Park Hospital, Surrey,

5. *28-30 May 2003: How to Practice Evidence-Based Care for Children.* Institute of Child Health, London.

6. *28-29 October 2002: **Third European Asthma Symposium**. London

7. *26-27 August 2001*: **Paediatric Advanced Life Support.** National Guard Hospital, Riyadh, KSA.

ADDITIONAL INFORMATION
- member of Diabetes UK and Asthma care UK
- skilled in using Microsoft Word and Powerpoint, and the internet.

HOBBIES
- Reading paediatric and medical literature on-line
- Charity work for Diabetes UK and Asthma Care UK

Mr S Chester FRCS

Address: 12 Hale Avenue
Millers Village
Catsford CZ2 5BH

Telephone: 0161 746 23x2 (day time)
Facsimile: 0161 972 011x (private)
e-mail: schester@catsford.nhs.uk

Name: **Samson CHESTER**
Date of birth: 15 June 1956
Nationality: British
Sex: Male.

PROFESSIONAL QUALIFICATIONS
FRCS 1990, Fellow of the Royal College of Surgeon of England.
MB ChB 1985, University of Manchester

PROFESSIONAL ORGANISATIONS
GMC Full Registration, on Specialist Register
Fellow of the Royal College of Surgeon of England.
Member of British Medical Association
Member of Medical Defence Union.

SKILLS AND ACHIEVEMENTS
- **Colorectal and general surgery**
  – serve as consultant general surgeon with interest in colorectal surgery
  – my team has improved 5-year survivals after colorectal surgery by **x%**

- **Service management**
- built an effective surgical team from a diversity of doctors and nurses that has improved 5-year survival after colorectal surgery by **x**% in 7 years.
- clinical director for general surgery and otorhinolaryngology

- **Clinical governance**
- ensure effective clinical care through training, use of guidelines and audit
- supervise junior doctors in clinical skills, writing notes, letters and reports
- with colleagues draft, test and regularly review local clinical guidelines.

- **Teaching**
- teach surgery to medical students, house officers and registrars.
- mentor immigrant doctors coming into the NHS; teach them how to write letters, curricula vitae and manage job interviews

- **Clinical Audit**
- skilled in performing clinical audits, writing reports and presenting them
- teach house officers and registrar clinical audit, and writing audit reports.

CURRENT EMPLOYMENT

From Nov. 1995: ***Consultant surgeon***, Catsford NHS Trust, Catsford:
- serve as consultant in general surgeon with interest in colorectal surgery
- my team has achieved 5 years survivals after colorectal surgery by **x**%
- supervise and teach medical students, senior house officers and registrars
- serve on trust's education, transfusion and medical advisory committees.

PREVIOUS EMPLOYMENT

Sept. 1991 – Nov 1995: ***Senior registrar in surgery***, North-West Regional Health Authority, rotated through hospitals in Greater Manchester
- ward rounds, clinics, operating sessions, night and week end on-call

– supervised and taught surgical skills to junior and senior house officers

*1989 – Aug 1991: **Registrar in surgery**,* Hope Hospital, Salford:
– hospital ward rounds, clinics, operative sessions, with on-calls
– supervised and taught surgical skills to junior and senior house officers

*Aug 1987 – Aug 1989: **Senior house officer in surgery**,* Wigan Infirmary
– hospital ward rounds, clinics, operative sessions, with on-calls

Aug 1986- Aug 1987: ***SHO in Emergency Medicine***, Preston Hospital, Preston:

*Aug 1985 – Aug 1986: **House Officer**,* Bolton General Hospital, Bolton
– Surgery (6 months) and Medicine (6 months).

PUBLICATIONS

1. Chester S. ***Impact of whole team training in surgical techniques on survival after colorectal surgery.*** *J Gut Surg* 1994; 67(2): 12-14

2. Chester S, Jones MT. **Predictive value of stool occult blood in colon cancer.** *J Gut Surg* 1994; 64(3): 95-97.

3. Chester S et al. ***CV format and short-listing rates among immigrant doctors.*** *J Med Experience* 1999; 3(2): 23-26.

4. Chester S et al. ***'Presentation' at consultant interviews and success as a surgeon.*** *J Med Recruitment* 2003; 5(3): 43-47.

HOBBIES
Swimming and Golf

Dr SJ Murphy Msc FRCP MBA

Address:	42 Hale Avenue
	Millers Village
	Catsford CZ2 5BH

Telephone:	011x 973 26x2 (work)
	077 5416 864x (mobile)
E-mail:	sandra.Murphy@catsford.nhs.uk

Name:	**Sandra Jane MURPHY**
Date of birth:	31 December 1956
Nationality:	British
Sex:	Female.

QUALIFICATIONS

MB ChB   1985, University of Liverpool, UK
MRCP(UK) 1988, Royal Colleges of Physician, UK
FRCP   1995, Royal College of Physician of London
MBA   2002, University of Durham (by distance learning).

PROFESSIONAL BODIES

Full registration with the General Medical Council
Fellow of the Royal College of Physicians of London
Member of British Association of Medical Managers

CAREER PLAN

I am seeking an opportunity to use skills gained from service as a senior clinician-manager in a strategic health care organisation.

EXPERIENCE AND SKILLS

- *General Medicine and diabetes*
  - clinical general medicine and diabetes practice for over 15 years
  - established a dedicated diabetes service with nurse specialists

- *Service leadership*
  - divisional director for medical specialties, deputy medical director
  - advise Catsford Community Health Council on clinical issues
  - developed clinical teams, facilitated change as chief of Medicine
  - MBA has given me insight into leading and motivating people

- *Clinical governance*
  - ensured the quality of personal and departmental clinical care
  - promoted the use of evidence based guidelines in patient care
  - lead for training in clinical governance and risk management.

- *Teaching*
  - lead for training in clinical governance and risk management.
  - BAMM faculty member on appraisal training for NHS doctors.
  - examiner in Medicine for the Royal Colleges of Physicians.

- *Clinical Audit*
  - supervise senior house officers and registrars in clinical audit
  - effected staff training in recognition and prevention of clinical risks
  - published articles on audit of diabetes care in Catsford.

EDUCATION

1980 – 1985: University of Liverpool Medical School (MB ChB studies)
- president of Liverpool Medical Students' Association (1984).

April 1998 - July 2002: MBA, Durham Business School, Durham, UK

– study by distance learning, annual summer school and written exams,
– MBA dissertation *"Barriers to high quality clinical services".*

CURRENT WORK

Oct 1997 – to date: **Consultant Physician,** Catsford NHS Trust, Catsford:
– acute hospital medicine and diabetes practice
– supervise and teach medical students and junior doctors
– divisional director for Medical specialties, deputy medical director.

Non-contractual health care activities
– medical adviser to Catsford branch of Diabetes UK
– appraiser of locum doctors for NHS Professionals
– faculty member on BAMM appraisal training.

WORK HISTORY

Sept. 1995 - Sep. 1996: **Senior Registrar in Medicine,** Catsford Hospitals;
rotated through medical subspecialties
– completed a study of the *"Consonance of knowledge among GPs and
  practice nurses on the importance of proteinuria in diabetes.*

July 1993 - Aug 1995: **Consultant Physician,** King Khalid Hospital, Hail,
KSA, employed by Global Health Ltd to establish regional diabetes services
– hospital general medicine, endocrinology and diabetes practice,
– established a hospital and then a regional diabetes service that trains
  and supervises nurses and doctors in distant hospitals and clinics
– taught clinical medicine and diabetes to staff physicians and nurses.

Aug 1990- June 1993: **Senior Registrar in Medicine** Catsford Infirmary
– hospital and ambulatory medical practice, and diabetology
– researched and published: *"Onset of neuropathy from in type 1 diabetes."*

April 1987- July 1990: **Registrar in Medicine,** Preston General Hospital
− medical ward rounds and outpatient clinics
− taught and supervised house officers and senior house officers

1986 - March 1987: **Senior house officer in Medicine,** Catsford Infirmary.
rotated through Neurology, Endocrinology, Chest medicine and Geriatrics.

Aug 1985 - July 1986: **Pre-registration House officer**, Catsford Infirmary
Catsford (Medicine and then Surgery).

PUBLICATIONS
1. Murphy SJ, et. al. **Onset of diabetic neuropathy in type 1 diabetes.**
   J Diabetes Medicine 1991; 5:231 - 232.

2. Murphy SJ. **Coping with diabetes.** Catsford: Livre Ltd 1993

3. Murphy SJ. **Concordance of a primary care team on urinalysis in diabetes nephropathy.** *J Prim health care* 1995; 34(6): 432-434.

4. Murphy SJ. **From clinician to manager.** Catsford: Livre Ltd 2003.

HOBBIES
1. Gardening and rambling
2. Political euphemisms.

2.14 Common mistakes in CVs

The following are errors commonly found in CVs:

- Too long, too fancy
- Badly set out, poorly typed
- Misspellings and/or bad grammar
- Disorganised, too many irregularities
- Too many obvious omissions
- Out of date or irrelevant details.

2.14.1 Too long

Your CV has one mission– to convey your suitability for a job to the recruiter. It is not the length, but the content that maters. If you follow '*Usual Format for Medical CVs,* by the time you have covered all the topics, your CV will be at least 2 typed A4 pages. If what is needed is in those pages then that is all you should write.

Of course after you have done several jobs and participated in teaching, committee work, done research, written and published articles, done clinical audit and participated in clinical governance, your CV will be long without being too long. It is your duty to write a *simple, clear* and *concise* CV.

2.14.2 Too fancy

Word processors and computers have made it too easy to vary the size of letters and their styles (fonts). Some doctors seem to be determined to include as many fonts as possible in their CV. They then enclose every heading in a 'box'.

While intended to impress, different letter sizes, fanciful fonts, excessive highlights outlining every heading, bullet points for every line result in bizarre documents.

The layout of your CV should make it easy to read and to locate information. The CV examples above use one size of letters, one font (Arial), capitals, bold letters and italics to create documents that are easy to read (so I hope).

Writing the medical CV

2.14.3 Misspellings and/or bad grammar

Your computer spellchecker will not distinguish between *they, their,* and *there.* It will accept *wear, were,* and *ware*; and other words with similar pronunciation, but different spelling and meaning. Only you, by reading your CV carefully, can ensure the right word has been used. There are no shortcuts to good grammar.

If you want to improve your grammar, help is available (at a small price):
- Strunk W, White EB. **The Elements of Style.** London: Longman 1999.
- Jarvie G. **Bloomsbury Grammar Guide.** London: Bloomsbury 2000.
- Ritter RM. *The Oxford Manual of Style.* London: BCA (Oxford UP) 2002.

2.14.4 Too many obvious omissions

I have read CVs in which applicants do not list qualifications, not even the MB ChB (BM BS). Often the university awarding the MB BS is not named.

State your qualifications, name the source of your degree (college, university). Other applicants will do. Why won't you?

Missing months and years

While a few weeks may not matter, gaps of several months or years will be noticed. Unexplained gaps invite speculation– *Was he sick, studying for exams, in prison...?* Mind the gaps! Explain significant gaps in your work history:
- preparing for and taking PLAB exams
- competing in the winter Olympic games
- full time study for an MSc in sports medicine, etc.

2.14.5 Disorganised, too many irregularities

Your CV should be easy to read. A disorganised and irregular document often results from not following standard typing conventions (mixing capitals and low case letters in lists or titles, irregular indentation and excess guttering).

Mixing capitals and low case letters

Capitals and lower case letters (**W** and **w**, **G** and **g**, **P** and **p**, etc.) are scattered throughout the CV. This is obvious in lists and titles. Examples:

Writing the medical CV

Summary
- think carefully of what to include or exclude from the CV
- Write a focused, clear, concise and simple CV
- use simple, short words and short sentences

Instead of:
- think carefully of what to include or exclude from the CV
- write a focused, clear, concise and simple CV
- use simple, short words and short sentences

Or:
- Think carefully of what to include or exclude from the CV
- Write a focused, clear, concise and simple CV
- Use simple, short words and short sentences.

*July199-June1998: **registrar in General paediatrics,** Wigan Infirmary*

Instead of:
*July 1997- June 1998: **Registrar in general paediatrics,** Wigan Infirmary,*

Or:
*July 1997- June 1998: **Registrar in General Paediatrics,** Wigan Infirmary.*

Irregular indentation
Uneven indentation creates a misaligned text on the left and makes the document look shabby.

Excess guttering on the left
An excessively wide margin (gutter), *as in this paragraph,* pushes the text to the right. What is the gutter for?

No gap between words and symbols
Omitting the normal space between words and symbols is common in CVs

written by novices. Example:

23June instead of **23 June**

Number:235 instead of **Number: 235**

No logical order

Although the information is in the CV, it is difficult to find. Career plans are mixed with skills, audit with hobbies, publications with research projects, etc.

2.14.6 Hiding experience acquired abroad

Some applicants minimise (almost hide) experience gain abroad. Perhaps they believe that it is not relevant to their future in the NHS. That is wrong. It is relevant and should be described properly. Recruiters want to know what you did before coming to the UK. Tell them in your CV.

I recall reading a young doctor's CV in which 12 months was unaccounted for. It turned out that he was on national service (working as a doctor in the army). Why was he ashamed of it? Later I learnt he had been advised to minimise or hide such experiences.

Over the years I found that talking about my experience abroad was easy and rewarding. Some interviewers liked it– a few took over the talking!

Describe your experience abroad clearly and concisely. Explain unusual titles (give British equivalents). Employers want to know what you did in the time between graduation and coming to the UK.

2.14.7 Out of date details

One SHO working in obstetrics and gynaecology submitted a CV for a job in paediatrics, in which the Career Plan stated that "after finishing house jobs I would like to work in Obstetrics and Gynaecology to gain accreditation for Family Planning". The doctor had not revised the CV prepared towards the end of the PRHO year before applying for the paediatrics post.

2.14.8 Do these errors matter?

Individually they are trivial faults, but if your CV contains several, it may fail in its mission– getting you short-listed for an interview. Therefore:

- keep your CV up to date; revise it before posting
- give all relevant information in a pleasing format
- ensure there are no unexplained gaps (time)
- check your spelling and grammar
- follow modern typing conventions.

Summary

- The job of a CV is to get you an interview with the employer/recruiter.

- Think carefully about what to include or exclude from the CV. No lies. However you should not volunteer unfavourable facts.

- Write a focused, clear, concise and simple CV. It should be well presented and easy to read. Untidy, poorly prepared CVs are rejected.

- Read the person and job specifications carefully and ensure your CV contains the qualifications, skills and experience required by the job.

- Ensure your qualifications, skills and clinical experience are easy to find. Give dates, job title, name of employer and summarise your responsibilities and achievements in each post, particularly the most recent.

- Give concise details of teaching experience, clinical audit, research, courses attended, and leadership skills (if you have them).

- If you qualified or have worked outside the UK describe your work experience abroad fully. Give the UK equivalents of unusual job titles.

- Describe postgraduate qualification gained abroad. Include the title of the dissertation or thesis for your MS, MD MMed or other degree. Describe research done abroad. List publications gained abroad in full.

- Choose your referees carefully and get their permission before naming them. Don't use people likely to give you bad references (if you want the job)

- Briefly describe your non-professional interests outside medicine. Present yourself as a competent, skilled worker with a normal life.

- Be prepared to discuss and clarify statements made in your CV. Do not include anything you are not happy to discuss at interview.

- Keep a copy of the CV you submit in application. You should have it to read before the interview (if short-listed!).

Update your CV regularly– you may need it sooner!

Further Reading

1. Eggert M. **The Perfect CV.** Arrow Business Books 1999.

2. Strunk W, White EB. **The Elements of Style.** London: Longman 1999.

3. Jarvie G. **Bloomsbury Grammar Guide.** London: Bloomsbury 2000.

4. Ritter RM. *The Oxford Manual of Style.* London: BCA for Oxford UP 2002.

5. Hutton-Taylor S. **Marketing yourself as an overseas doctor.** *BMJ* 2002; 324: s75

6. GMC. Case Book: **Doctor suspended after making false claims.** GMC News 14 October 2002. www.gmc-uk.org

---

3. Applying for jobs

Applying for jobs

3.1 Which specialty?

If you are newly registered qualified doctor or have just passed PLAB, how do you decide on the medical specialty to pursue? Will it be surgical, medical, laboratory medicine, general practice or other community based specialty?

Do you enjoy all specialties equally and will drift from post to post? What factors do you consider when choosing a specialty?

3.1.1 What do you want from your career?

Think about what you want to gain from your career before asking for advice from others:

- Why did you study medicine?
- What would be your ideal specialty?
- Do you like working with your hands, discussing things or both?
- Do you like working with groups, interacting with different people?
- Are there factors that would make some specialties unsuitable?
- Do you/would you have access to training and clinical experience?
- What qualifications and experience do you need for the specialty?
- Are you free (of dependants' needs) to pursue your ideal specialty?

3.1.2 What do you enjoy doing?

Doing the work you enjoy is very important. Do not be persuaded, seduced into a specialty that you do not like or enjoy. You need to mix the hard work of medical practice with enthusiasm and fun. At the end of the day/shift/night on-call you should feel that you have given a useful service to those who needed your help, and enjoyed the work.

While some doctors thrive on stress, others prefer quieter work-lives. Although doctors in general enjoy contact with patients, some prefer the challenges of laboratory medicine, medical research or public health.

Whatever your inclination you need to choose your specialty carefully. Changing course after several years in specialty X is painful and may be viewed suspiciously by some employers.

Can you find an informed advisor to help you:
- Obtain information on specialty requirements and job prospects
- Clarify advantages and disadvantages of different specialties
- Decide between hospital medicine and general practice
- Ascertain your personal suitability for a specialty
- Pick a particular specialty or subspecialty
- Explore career options outside medicine.

3.1.3 Career prospects

For many reasons, some specialties are easier to enter than others. Job prospects are difficult to predict and the popularity of disciplines changes every few years almost randomly. Be realistic about opportunities in competitive specialties and about your qualifications compared with those of the competition.

At the moment (2004), competition for senior house officer and registrar jobs is harshest in surgery, general medicine, emergency medicine and paediatrics. There is a shortage of general practitioners, consultants in psychiatry, anaesthesia, histopathology and radiology; but SHO posts are scarce in anaesthesia, emergency medicine, and histopathology.

The situation changes quickly and you should keep an eye on the demand and supply of SpR, GP registrar as well as consultant and GP principal posts as necessary. Do not get so fixated on one specialty that you wouldn't consider openings in other disciplines.

Foreign doctors have traditionally found work in less popular disciplines. In the 1970 and 1980s, these were general practice, pathology, geriatrics (care of the elderly), community child health and family planning. The picture has changed. Many community units (child health and family planning) have been integrated with their hospital cousins or into primary care. Keep yourself informed.

3.1.4 Find an adviser

It may be beneficial to speak to somebody you already know so that the advice can be tailored to your personal circumstances. However, a new adviser may be more impartial. If you have narrowed your choice of specialty to a few, find an adviser from each of those specialties. He/she should have the knowledge and experience to give you detailed advice.

Ask colleagues to put you in touch with individuals from whom they have received impartial and valuable advice.

Inform your adviser of your career aims, achievements to date, perceived weaknesses and strengths. State the specific nature of the advice you seek before the meeting. This will allow her/him to look into relevant issues or to refer you to a more appropriate person.

Arrange not to be disturbed during the meeting. Be clear and concise about the help you seek, the choices you have already made and the specialties you do not wish to pursue. Write down important suggestions so that you can reflect on them later.

It is often difficult to decide whether to follow or reject advice. Do not reject unpalatable advice out of hand. Ask yourself if the advisor could be right. Did he/she give reasons for the advice? Does it fit personal circumstances? Does it agree with advice from others, including those who are already in the discipline? Thank the advisor for meeting you and tell her/him how useful the meeting was.

3.1.5 Variety, excitement and tedium

Medical practice means seeing patients with the same conditions over and over, repeating procedures and giving the same explanations or similar advice repeatedly. It is unlike medical school where learning new things is the norm. Graduation gave you an entry ticket into the world of unavoidable repetition. That is why your choice is important– to secure you 'repeats' you will still enjoy.

I remember, as an SHO in Medicine, working with Mark, a PRHO. He was bright and ambitious. He knew more syndromes than I did. However there was no opportunity to study the syndromes beyond clerking patient after patient and collecting blood sample after blood sample. The tedium got him. He lost interest and left in his 3rd month of medical practice.

Some specialities have more variety than others. Emergency medicine is possibly the least predictable. However some doctors want something less exciting than A & E. The choice is wide– hospital medical, surgical, general practice, psychiatry, laboratory medicine, community medicine and public health, pharmaceutical medicine, and managerial (for more senior doctors).

3.1.6 Getting further advice

Advice on medical specialism is available from royal medical colleges and their faculties, postgraduate deans, postgraduate tutors, regional advisors, and college advisors. If you are not familiar with these organisations or offices, ask you senior colleagues, the medical librarian or your clinical tutor.

The best advice, probably, will come from those who are already established in specialties you are considering. Many of them will be happy to discuss the advantages and disadvantages of their disciplines. They may also direct you to the more appropriate sources of information.

Your choice will make the difference between 30 years of enjoyment and 30 years of drudgery. Think carefully before you decide on a specialty.

3.2 At what level?

Doctors who have passed PLAB find it difficult to decide the level at which to seek employment in the NHS. It is unlikely that a consultant from a non-European Union or North American country will find work in the NHS at the same level, unless he has EU qualifications– then he/she would not need PLAB! Most, if not all PLAB graduates enter the NHS at SHO; sometimes at HO level.

Has he worked in the UK before?

Some recruiters want to know if the doctor has *"worked in the UK"* before. PLAB graduates who do HO jobs in UK sometimes get SHO jobs ahead of those that have not. Those with postgraduate qualifications from their native countries (e.g. MD from India) may have an advantage if the training and dissertation are properly described in the CV.

3.3 Which job?

The entry level is determined by experience:

- a *new graduate* has to complete the compulsory pre-registration year; so the choice is between hospitals and their departments– how good is the hospital, how good is the supervision, how heavy is the workload...?

- a *newly registered doctor* must chose between career paths– hospital medicine or general practice, community health, abandon medicine?

- a *senior house officer* must choose between specialties– medical, surgical, general practice, psychiatry, pathology, public health...?

- a *young specialist doctor* must chose jobs according to reputation of hospital/PCT, its clinical teams and managers.

- a *senior doctor*'s *choice* will be influenced by the need to change jobs, or find new opportunities (clinical, research, teaching, managerial), a wish to change the work environment, better pay and or working conditions....

3.4 Finding medical jobs

Most medical jobs are advertised in *BMJ Careers* and on **www.bmj.com.**
Medical jobs also appear on other websites including:

The Lancet Interactive	www.thelancet.com/
NHS Professionals	www.nhsprofessionals.nhs.uk/
PersonnelNet Health	www.personnelnet.co.uk/
Artemis Executive jobs search	www.artemis-europe.com/
Health Service Journal	www.hsj.co.uk/

3.4.1 Locum agencies

Locum agencies help doctors find temporary work. They usually charge the employer (hospital or GP practice) a fee for the service. You are paid more for accepting a locum job through an agency than taking it directly from the hospital's medical staffing department. I do not understand the economics. I gave up trying to understand NHS logic many years ago!

3.4.2 Networking/ word of mouth

Friends or other contacts may have information about jobs− good jobs. Ask them to tell you of interesting jobs they hear about. Develop a linked group (network) of individuals who will tell you of coming openings. This is called *networking.* Most executive post are filled through networking; some never get advertised.

3.4.3 Headhunting

Head hunters are agents who earn their living by finding scarce executives, specialist and other workers for organisation that need the workers but are unable or do not want to do their own searches.

The head hunter approaches the target worker and persuades him/her to change employers for better rewards. Scarce consultants are sometimes head hunted to leave one NHS trust for another at salary premiums.

You have to be pretty good, one of a few of your kind, to be headhunted.

3.5 Should you apply?

When you apply for a job, the question asked about you is: *Is he/she the right doctor for the job?* Will she do the job willingly? Will she fit into the clinical team?

Let us assume you are looking for a PRHO, HO, SHO or other job. You have found an interesting advert *on www.bmj.com:*

• What do you do next? *Contact the advertiser for a job description. You have read the job description. Do you have the qualifications– person specifications (qualifications, experience, skills and other attributes)?*

• Do you like the job (the duties and responsibilities)?

Look at your qualifications and skills
• Are your skills adequate for the job?
• Are you aiming too high or too low?

Before applying for a job, ensure that you like the post– hospital, PCT, GP practice or other health care organisation. Read the job description and person specification again.

Talk to people in the post/organisation
• What is good and not so good about the post?
• How good is the hospital/ trust/ quango?
• Are the nurses and consultants friendly?
• Are the managers humane or robotic?
• How reputable is the organisation?
• Are you comfortable working with those guys?
• Does the department teach for membership exams?
Etc.

Now you are in a position to *think about applying.* If you decide to apply, how shall you convince the recruiter that you are the right doctor/executive?

Send them your best CV and Letter of application; or a carefully completed application form. Ensure that your application works for you. Provide them with evidence that you are the answer to their needs. Help them conclude that: *"This is the right doctor."*

3.6 Application forms

Some employers insist on completed application forms. A few recruiters (university hospitals usually) want completed application forms and CVs.

Organise your information before completing the form. Your CV should contain sorted information, ready to be transferred to the applications form. You can practice on a photocopy before completing the original.

Complete the form carefully with black ink. If your handwriting is poor, write in clear CAPITAL letters. Be careful with capitals– they can look untidy and may be difficult to read. Answer every questions even if it means writing **'No, Nil,** or **Not applicable'** many times.

If asked to "apply in your own handwriting", make sure you are able to write neatly (pen, mood, lighting, furniture and posture). Have you heard of character analysis from handwriting? This is said to occur in business recruitment, but apparently not in the NHS– yet.

3.7 Will a letter do?

If asked to apply in writing, you should send your best CV and a typed letter of application (see 4.0: *Letter of application*), written specifically to address the job and person specifications *(qualifications, experience and skills the ideal candidate would have)* for the post. An ordinary letter is not enough.

Will a letter do?

Dr James Ngaka
PO Box 456
Maseru 100
Lesotho.

7 November 2003

Dr Paul Orchard
Maudsley Hospital
Denmark Hill
London SE5 8AZ

Dear Dr Orchard

Re: Application for an SHO post in psychiatry

I wish to apply for the senior house officer post in psychiatry in your hospital advertised on www.bmj.com on 5 November 2003.

I am a 31year old graduate of the University of Cape Town. I have been working in psychiatry at Queen Elizabeth II Hospital, Maseru for 5 years.

Thank you for your assistance in getting me a training post in psychiatry in your reputable hospital.

Yours faithfully,

JNgaka
James Ngaka MB ChB

Dr Ngaka's application *(above)* does not anticipate basic questions:
- What is his experience outside psychiatry?
- How long has he worked in psychiatry?
- Does he have any hobbies?
- Who are his referees?

He could have volunteered answers to these and other questions by enclosing a CV with his letter. In a CV you can give a detailed summary of your career-listing information that would make a letter rather long and boring. What looks right and proper in a CV can look out of place in a letter.

A CV should always be accompanied by a relevant letter of application.
An application form too should be escorted back by a letter of application.

3.8 Do they want a CV?
If asked to send a CV, send a clean, current CV. Do you have a current well crafted, typed CV? If not then read chapter 2: *'Writing a winning CV'.* If your CV is out of date, revise it.

If you are applying for a managerial position, you will need to highlight different aspects of your skills and experience.

For senior doctors the CV on its own is not enough. It should be escorted by a focused letter of application. The letter should address person specifications one by one and show that you meet them very well.

3.9 New CV for each post?
Yes, ideally. However for most HO and SHO jobs, a good CV, revised before the next round of applications is enough. But you should write a new letter of application for each post *(see* chapter 4: *Letter of application).*

Senior doctors (specialist registrars, associate specialists, consultants and GP principals) should rewrite the CVs for each application they apply for– rather recast the information to address the job and person descriptions of each post.

3.10 Submitting your CV

Do not send you your CV by e-mail or fax. The quality of printer and paper used may not be impressive. The copy seen by the recruiter may be a poor version of the original document. This could ruin the impression you worked so hard to create. If the format of your document is incompatible with the recruiter's computer, the pages received could be unintelligible.

If you must send the document by e-mail then send it as an attachment to the e-mail. Send a letter of application as an attachment too. Immediately send printed copies by normal post. Sure, it is overkill!

Send copies of your CV to your referees to remind them of who you are and of your good work under their supervision. Junior doctors come and go every six months. Some consultants need reminding of who you are, when you worked with them and the highlights of your stay in their department. It is wise to tell them which job(s) you are applying for.

3.11 Testimonials

A testimonial is commendation written by referee that a candidate keeps with him and might send off with a CV or a completed application form.

Testimonials are less influential than confidential references. Generally UK employers do not accept testimonials as references. They prefer to contact your referees confidentially. Naturally nobody sends out a bad testimonial!

3.12 References

References are frequently obtained by telephone, fax and e-mail. So, include referees' telephone and fax numbers and e-mail address in your CV or the letter of application. The recruiter can then obtain your references quickly (in hours rather than days). Get permission before naming anybody as a referee.

Summary
- Written applications may be made by either:
- – a relevant, neat, typed CV and a letter of application; **or**
- – a completed application form and a letter of application.

- Sometimes a completed application form *and* a CV are requested. You should send a letter of application too.

- Send copies of your CV to your referees to remind them of who you are and of your good work under their supervision.

- Send your application early. It must arrive before the closing date.

Do not send the originals of your documents unless specifically asked. Your prized certificate could get lost.

Further reading

1. Hutton-Taylor S. **Marketing yourself as an overseas doctor.** *BMJ* 2002; 324:s75

2. Beatty R. **The Perfect Cover Letter**. New York: Wiley 1997.

3. Burnet S. **How to get short listed.** *BMJ* 2002; 324: s3

6. Peskett *S*, Empey *D*. **A career check for medical managers.** BMJ 2003; 327: s179- s180

---

4 Letter of application

Letter of application

4.1 What is a letter of application?

For registrar and more senior positions, the Letter of Application (Cover Letter) is almost as important as the CV or application form. The letter:

- highlights your suitability for the post
- introduces your CV or application from to the recruiter
- invites the recruiter to read your CV or application.

4.2 Length of letter of application *(= one side of A4 page)*

The letter of application should be one typed page (one side of an A4 page). Edit your letter till it is *concise* and *simple*– then it will fit onto the single page. Its layout should signpost important details– your qualifications, experience, skills and other attributes.

4.3 Write to a named person

Write to the individual or office responsible for recruiting. Adverts for medical jobs usually give the name or title of the person to contact. Include the officer's name and title; if you do not have the name, use the title.

Follow the structure for letters discussed in chapter 1: *Writing Effective Letters*. Give full contact details so that the recruiter can reach you either by post, telephone, fax or e-mail.

4.4 Name the post, quote its reference number

Naming the post and quoting the reference number ensures that your letter and CV go to the right department and consultant(s). The hospital may be recruiting for different jobs of the same grade.

4.5 Summarise your competencies

Summarise a few skills and achievements (clinical, leadership, teaching, clinical audit) to illustrate your suitability for the job.

End with *'Yours sincerely'* (if you used the officer's name) or *'Yours faithfully'* (if an official title only was used). Sign, and print your name bellow the signature.

4.6 Letters from junior doctors

4.5.1.1. Dr Smyth, seeks a SHO post on surgical training rotation

4.5.1.2. Dr Shastri has passed PLAB and wants an SHO post

4.5.1.3. Dr Chieke, a LAT Registrar, seeks an SpR training rotation.

4.5.1.1. Dr Smyth seeks a SHO post on surgical training rotation

Dr R Smyth MB ChB
231 Seymour Grove
Old Trafford
Manchester M16 0LW

Tel 0161 5643 76xx
077 5416 x61x
rsmyth@hotmail.com

19 January 2004

Medical Staffing Department
University Hospitals North Staffordshire
Princes Road
Hartshill
Stoke on Trent
Staffordshire ST4 7LN

Re: Application for post of Senior House Officer, Basic Surgical Rotation

May I apply for a senior house officer post on your Basic Surgical Rotation advertise on www.bmj.com on 15 January 2004.

I passed part 1 MRCS in April 2003 and hope to join a surgical training rotation, complete MRCS exams in 2005, and specialise in orthopaedics.

I am skilled in using Microsoft Word, Excel and Power Point, internet searches and desktop publishing.

Details of my employment history, clinical audit and names of my referees are included in the enclosed completed application form and curricula vitae.

Yours faithfully

RSmyth
Dr. R Smyth MB ChB

4.5.1.2. Dr Shastri has passed PLAB and wants an SHO post

Dr Indra Shastri MD
218 Moorside Rd
Urmston
Manchester M41 5SL

Tel. 0161 747 976x
Indra65@hotmail.com

22 November 2003

The Personnel Officer
Bradford Royal Infirmary
Duckworth Lane
Bradford BD9 6RJ

Re: Application for post of Senior House Officer in Obstetrics and Gynaecology (Ref AOG 357).

I would like to apply the post of Senior House Officer in Obstetrics and Gynaecology advertised in the BMJ, 14 November 2003.

I have an MD in Obstetrics and Gynaecology, passed PLAB in June and Part 1 MRCOG in September 2003.

After obtaining the MRCOG, I hope to spend 2 years as registrar in gynaecological surgery before returning to work in Kerela, India.

Details of my qualifications, clinical experience, publications and referees are shown in the enclosed curriculum vitae.

Yours faithfully

IShastri
Dr Indra Shastri MB BS MD

4.5.1.3. Dr Chieke, a LAT Registrar, seeks an SpR training rotation.

17 Campion Close
Eccleshall
Stafford ST21 6SR

Tel: 077 374x44
echieke@yahoo.co.uk

12 October 2002

Miss Patricia Matthews
Catsford Deanery
Catsford House
Catsford CZ76 5PQ

Dear Miss Matthews

Re: Application for the SpR post in Medicine, M213

May I apply for one the advertised posts of Specialist Registrar in Medicine? I have the skills and knowledge to perform the duties and learn from the post.

I have a wide experience in *tropical medicine* and infectious diseases, and *general medicine* (cardiology, endocrinology, gastroenterology nephrology and respiratory).

I have *taught* medical students and senior house officers using didactic and problem based learning methods.

I have done some *research and clinical audit,* presented the results and published some in peer reviewed journals.

Leadership skills come from service as secretary of Benin University Students Union and current service on my department's 'clinical governance committee'.

A copy of my curriculum vitae is enclosed.

Yours sincerely,

ℰChieke

Ebele Chieke MB ChB MRCP

4.7 Letters from senior doctors

A letter of application (cover letter) from a senior doctor (consultant, medical manager, GP principal) should show an appreciation of the difference between applications for clinical posts and those for managerial roles.

> *".... the all important covering letter, needs to be tailor made for the job. It needs to be ruthlessly proactive: you should emphasise your main competencies (you probably have many, but highlight no more than five). It also needs to be reactive: you must show how you match their needs as set out in the person specification and not just ramble on about your own view of yourself".* (Peskett & Empey BMJ 2003;327:s179-s180)

Most senior doctors apply for jobs by returning a completed application form or by sending off the CV and brief note indicating the post they seek. They do not sell themselves through a letter as well. Drs Peskett and Empey emphasise the importance of a cover letter and that it should be used to show you have the desired competencies.

For managerial posts the letter is as important as the CV or application form; perhaps more important– it entices the recruiter to study the CV. If she is not impressed by the letter, it is unlikely the applicant will be short listed.

The following examples demonstrate how a letter of application can be used to bring out your strong points– to sell you skills. Dr Murphy is applying for a managerial role, so her letter is qualitatively different from those of Dr Walker and Dr Khan who are applying for traditional consultant posts:

4.5.2 1. Dr Walker, a recent SpR, seeks a consultant post
4.5.2 2. Dr Khan, a locum consultant, wants a substantive post
4.5.2 3. Dr Murphy aims for medical director of a quango.

4.5.2.1. Dr. Walker, a recent SpR, seeks a consultant post

Dr AP Walker MRCPCH
112 Park Road
Altrincham WA15 5AB

Tel: 077912367x6
apwalker@hotmail.com

2 November 2003

The Recruitment Administrator
Stepping Hill Hospital
Poplar Grove
Stockport SK2 7JE

Re: Application for the post of Consultant Paediatrician Ref 875/03/FMS.

May I apply for the advertised post of consultant paediatrician in hospital and community paediatrics. I have the skills to perform the duties effectively.

I have worked in *general and neonatal paediatrics* for 12 years (7 years at registrar level, 5 years after the MRCPCH

The MSc in *community paediatrics* introduced me to epidemiology, public health policy, and performance measurement. Formal SpR training included child protection, developmental delay, adoption and fostering and behavioural paediatrics.

Leadership skills come from captaincy of school soccer team, organising teaching for senior house officers and serving on the hospital *"hospital at night"* committee.

Details of my qualifications, experience and names of my referees are shown on enclosed application form.

Yours sincerely
QP Walker
Dr. A P Walker MSc MRCPCH

4.5.2.2. Dr M A Khan, a locum consultant, seeks a substantive post

Dr M A Khan FRCPCH
19 Cromwell Rd
Romford RM1 2RP

Mobile: 07952 7451X7
makhan54@hotmai.com

11 January 2004

Chris Bates
Medical Personnel Officer
North Devon District Hospital
Raleigh Park, Barnstaple
Devon EX31 4JB

Dear Chris Bates

Re: Application for post of Acute Consultant Paediatrician

I would like to apply for one of the Acute Consultant Paediatrician posts at North Devon District Hospital advertised on www.bmj.com, 08 January 2004

I am on the specialist register as a general paediatrician. I have an interest in diabetes and would be happy to lead clinician in *Diabetes.*

As clinical director of a multinational paediatrician team, I led on clinical audit and medical education, and served on pharmacy committees.

I address clinical governance through training, use of guidelines and clinical audit.

I have the skills essential in an Acute Consultant Paediatrician in a general hospital.

A copy of my curriculum vitae with names of my referees is enclosed.

Yours sincerely

MAKhan

Dr MA Khan FRCPCH

Writing the medical CV

4.5.2.3. Dr JS Murphy wants to be a medical director at an NHS quango

Dr. J S Murphy FRCP MBA
42 Hale Avenue
Catsford CZ2 5BH

Tel 077 5416 864x
Fax 011x 973 2646x
sandra.murphy@catsford.nhs.uk

24 January 2004

Mr Peter Savage
The Chief Executive
PatientConcern
23 Barclay Square
Catsford CZ6 4BE

Dear Mr Savage

Re: Application for Post of Medical Director at PatientConcern

May I apply for the post of medical director at PatientConcern advertised in Hospital Service Journal? I have the skills for an effective medical director at PatientConcern.

My experience in *service management and leadership* includes serving as divisional director and deputy medical director of hospital trust. I was on clinical governance to Catsford Community Health Council for 5 years.

I manage *clinical governance* and by promoting the using clinical guideline, regular clinical audits and sharing of experience through biannual trust audit meetings. I promote regular training to maintain, or develop new clinical and managerial skills.

Details of my achievements work and my referees are shown on enclosed CV

Yours sincerely

JS Murphy

Dr J S Murphy FRCP MBA

Summary

- The letter of application:
- – introduces your CV or application from to the recruiter
- – concisely highlight the candidate's suitability for the post
- – entices the recruiter to study the application or read the CV.

- The letter must be limited to one page (one side of an A4 page):
- – write to the individual or official responsible for recruiting
- – name the post and quote its reference number to ensure that the application goes to the right consultant/senior executive.

- Address the job and person specifications– meet the recruiter needs– summarise your competencies and highlighting only skills and achievements relevant to the post.

- End with *'Yours sincerely'* (if an officer's name was used to start of the letter) or *'Yours faithfully'* (if an official title only was used).

- Sign the letter above your printed name.

Further reading

1. Hutton-Taylor S. **Marketing yourself as an overseas doctor.** *BMJ* 2002; 324:s75

2. Beatty R. **The Perfect Cover Letter**. New York: Wiley 1997.

3. Burnet S. **How to get short listed.** *BMJ* 2002; 324: s3

4. Peskett *S,* Empey *D.* **A career check for medical managers.** BMJ 2003; 327: s179- s180

---

5. Managing Interviews

Managing Interviews

5.1 What is an interview?

An interview is the occasion when two parties (individuals or groups) meet, view and talk with each other. In job searches this is when an applicant (interviewee) is seen (viewed) and questioned by interviewer(s) to determine her/his suitability for a job.

An interview is the opportunity for a doctor to meet and talk with recruiters (consultants, principal GPs or managers) with jobs to give away. The doctor's aim is to convince interviewers that he/she is the best there is and so they should give her/him the job and not someone else.

5.2 What are interviews for?

Several applicants, who meet the person specifications, are short-listed and interviewed to select the most suitable.

Can this doctor do the job? Usually only candidates with the desired qualifications are called for interview. What needs to be decided is:

Is he/she the right person for the job?
Does he have the right personality and drive? Is this the right job for his/her qualifications and skills? An applicant may not get the job because the interviewer thinks he would be better employed in a different capacity.

Is he/she suitable?
A sole applicant would not be appointed if he was not *suitable* for the post. He/she might have the diplomas and years of experience but still be

unsuitable— personality, demeanour, timidity, etc.

Will he/she do the job?

Is she willing to meet the needs of the job? If a doctor creates the impression that although capable, she could refuse to do the job, she will not be appointed.

Will he fit in?

People want somebody who will fit in nicely. Interviewers must satisfy themselves that *the appointed candidate was the most suitable.*

5.3 Pre-interview enquiries

Candidates for senior jobs— specialist registrar, consultant and GP principal are expected to visit the hospital or practice before they apply for the post, and often before interview.

Preparation for the interview is crucial, looking at areas of obvious relevance to the post and ordering your thoughts on the main topics. Peskett & Empey, *BMJ 2003; 327:s179-s180.*

Candidates for PRHO and SHO jobs are not normally expected to, but should speak to post incumbents. They should telephone and speak with the doctor doing the job who should be able to describe the job. The incumbent may also tell them about the staff (nurses, consultants, registrars and others). What is it like to work with them?

- Is the hospital friendly?
- Is the department friendly?
- What are the teaching arrangements?
- Do consultants teach for membership exams?

If you visit, you should:

- Look over as much of the organisation as possible (wards, library, doctor on-call rooms, doctors' mess, restaurant, local town, roads, cinema, etc.)

- Speak to doctors doing the job you want. Is it educational, enjoyable, or exhausting? Ask searching questions and listen to the answers. Discuss the duties; what will the employer expect of you?

- Speak to consultants and nurses about the post and related issues. Are they welcoming? You will work with them if you get the job!

If you inquiring about a *permanent* post check the neighbourhood– essential services (schools, shopping, entertainment, roads, airports) social biases, etc.

It is expected for an applicant for consultant post to meet the chief executive of the trust. Carefully enquire about clinician- manager relationships.
- Is the chief executive approachable?
- Does he welcome clinicians to discuss problems?

It is wise to tactfully explore the degree of collegiality among consultants and among consultant and managers in the department, the hospital and trust. Do they have a team spirit or are individual consultants isolated?

This is the time to satisfy yourself that you like the job, the place, and the people, and understand what is expected of you.

5.4 Preparing for interview

Before the interview, review your feelings about the post, the hospital, the department and the environment. Read the job and person specification again to ensure that your answers are relevant. Do you still want the job?

Are you ready to talk about your education, work history, skills and hobbies smoothly and confidently? It would be a shame if you did not remember the contents of your CV. Before the interview read a copy of the CV sent to apply for the job or used to complete the application form. Your interviewers will have copies of your CV or completed form in front of them, and will ask you about its contents.

Let us list a few questions commonly asked at interviews. How would you answer them?
– Why did you apply for this job?
– What are your career objectives?
– What are your weaknesses/strengths?

Clinical issues

- Tell us about your recent clinical audit.
- In your own words, what is clinical governance ?
- What is risk management? Can you give examples?
- Tell us about an interesting case you have dealt with recently
- What is the most challenging clinical situation you have handled?
- Tell me about your last audit (or research project).

Topical managerial issues

At interview for an SHO post or its equivalents, you are unlikely to be asked questions about topical medical, social and political debates of the day. If you are interviewing for a senior post (registrar, GP principal, consultant or clinician-manager) you will be asked a few.

How would you respond to: *"What do you think about…Tell me about…What are your views on:*
- continuous professional development
- appraisal and revalidation of doctors
- the European working time directive
- charging social services for bed blockers
- PCTs and commissioning health care
- the private finance initiative
- privately operated surgical centres
- clinical governance and risk management
Et cetera.......

A potential registrar or consultant should be able to say something intelligible on these and other socio-medico-political issues. It is worth your effort learning a bit about topical socio-medical issues. Medicine is practised in an environment governed by social attitudes and political directives. Politicians determine health care management structures, funding levels and priorities.

5.5 Presenting for interview

You are mentally ready. You have your certificates, identity papers and the invitation to the interview. What have you forgotten?

What will you *look* like *(appearance, confidence and personality)*; *sound* like *(voice, language, knowledge and tone of voice)?*

Often critical decisions *(Yes- no, Trust- Distrust, Love- Hate, Good- Bad,* etc.) are made after brief encounters (interviews). You meet him and in a few moments, you dislike him. He has failed the interview!

Normally only applicants with the right qualifications are invited for interview. So it is not lack of qualifications but rather the *impression* you create− your *appearance, speech, confidence* and *personality* that decides whether you get the job or not. Create a good impression and you may get the job. *Interviews are won or lost on impressions.*

5.5.1 Personal papers

Take your certificates, identification, GMC registration or legibility for registration, Hepatitis B immune status and other relevant documents with you. If you are successful, the medical staffing officer will want to check them.

5.5.2 Appearance

Your appearance will contribute to your performance at the interview. You should wear smart, clean and socially appropriate clothes. These should be items you are comfortable in− clothes you have worn before, that complement your body, and look good (neat, clean and pressed).

Do not wear clothes that make you uncomfortable. If you are uncomfortable you will fidget and give a poor impression.

I usually wear my best and most comfortable pants, trousers, shirt, jacket and shoes. I talk better if I am not being strangled by a tight collar, squeezed by a jacket too small for my chest or a pair of trousers that threatens to split into two each time I shift my buttocks.

Wear clothes that suit the position you seek. Think of the age and potential biases of your interviewers. Wear clothes that are unlikely to offend their sense of propriety. Some fashions are more acceptable than others irrespective of quality (and cost).

A standard shirt is more acceptable that a T-shirt. Jeans (denim) are unacceptable; wear standard trousers. Females tend to wear skirts and browses; trousers are now acceptable. Business suits are now routine among women in management or senior clinical positions. It is safer to wear little or no jewellery than to carry excess heavy metal!

It is difficult to predict what will annoy an interviewer. Senior doctors are more conservative than the general public. It may be safer to be conservative in your clothes. If you look young for your age, adopt the fashions that make you look a bit older but not elderly. Dress for a serious professional interview and not for a young people's party.

A senior doctor interviewing for managerial role would be expected to dress appropriately. His/her brief case, if one is carried, should be appropriate too— not the old thing you use haul patient files around clinics.

Is your *hair groomed, fingernails trimmed and clean. Are your shoes in good repair and shined?* Have you bathed? It would be a shame if you offended the interviewer's nose. Better not to smoke before the interview.

I know very little about perfumes. However a candidate who smelled like a perfume factory would not impress many interviewers. Use light perfume; and only if you normally use the stuff and know what is good.

5.5.3 Politeness

On arrival at the place of interview, speak and make your inquiries politely. You never know who is looking and listening. Do not offend any body. You could meet them again in the interview room! Bosses do not have to be behind big desks before they start interviewing you (*watching, listening and talking to you*). Keep alert and polite throughout the interview until you have left the premises.

When you enter the interview room wait till asked to sit. Then sit right into the chair with you back supported by back of the chair. Adjust your position if necessary till you are comfortable. Do not sit on the edge and risk falling off. Sit up, and remain attentive. Look at each member of the panel as he/she is introduced to you.

5.5.4 Behaving during the interview

* Smile; it is allowed, laugh appropriately
* Do tell the truth; it is easier to talk about
* Speak clearly, succinctly, give full answers.

* Do not draw attention to your weaknesses
* Do not criticise your previous employer
* Do not smoke, even if invited to
* Do not interrupt the interviewer
* Do not argue with the interviewer
* Do not get too familiar or personal.

5.5.5 Confidence and Personality

Your confidence and personality will be judged from your grooming, dress, composure, mannerisms, and speech. Your confidence is improved by how well you have prepared for the interview. You portray your best personality if you are well dressed, polite and speak clearly, audibly and knowledgeably.

5.5.6 Body language

Avoid annoying mannerisms (picking your nose, yawning, clicking your knuckles, constantly clearing your throat, etc). Do not give the impression that you do not care about the outcome of the interview. Keep interested and alert.

5.5.7 Speech

We speak to convey information, to be understood. So when you answer questions, *speak so that your answer is heard clearly and understood.* You should neither whisper nor shout.

Watch interviewers' faces to see if they hear and understand your answers. Your purpose is to convince them to give the job to you. If they cannot hear you well, they will not know how good you are. Look at each interviewer eye-to-eye for brief moments. Move your attention to the person speaking to you and listen. Understand the question before answering it. If it is not clear, ask him or her to explain it. *Speak clearly, concisely, and simply.*

Do not use jargon or abbreviations unless you are sure the interviewers know them too. Use ordinary words and language. Answer the question asked. Be *clear, brief* and *informative* in your answers. Give your answers politely and confidently. If you don't know say so clearly and confidently.

If an interviewer is talking do not interrupt. Let him talk. Listen and be ready to answer the question that will follow the speech.

5.6 Questions about the past

Sometimes candidates are asked about past failures. Be prepared to talk about something that did not turn out well. Talk about failure whose cause was identified, lessons learnt and which you are now able to discuss calmly and rationally. Stress the lessons and not the failure. Give one example only. You do not want to dwell on failure.

5.7 Do you have any questions?

Usually before the interview is concluded a candidate is asked if he/she has any questions. You do not have to ask questions. But if you have genuine questions ask them. Do not ask irrelevant questions; or questions whose answers were given to you a moment before. If you have no questions, thank the panel for the opportunity.

Summary

- Is it the right job, should you apply for the job?
- If you cannot visit, speak with the post incumbent?
- Complete the application form with black ink legibly and fully
- Send your CV or completed form and a letter of application
- Are your ready to answer questions (*on work, skills, audits, etc.*)?
- Are you physically prepared *(dress, bearing, speech, etc.)?*
- Do you look right (*dress, confidence, disposition, language*)?
- Are you mentally ready (*calm, confident and attentive*)?
- Do you have the appropriate documents?

Relax and do your best.

Further reading

1. Sudlow M, Toghill P. **How to be interviewed.** *BMJ* 1996; 313: 2.

2. Spillane M. **Branding Yourself:** how to look, sound and behave your way to success. Pan Macmillan: London 2000

3. Burnet S. **How to perform well at your interview.** *BMJ* 2002; 324: S69

4. Peskett S, Empey D. *A career check for medical managers.* BMJ 2003; 327:s179- s180

6. Growing your CV

Growing your CV

6.1 Desirable competencies

Your curriculum vitae (CV) summarises your professional attributes and work history. Its job is to tell potential employers what a good doctor you are– to get you interviews.

While most doctors leave the growth of their CVs to chance, others actively influence the development of the vital self-marketing tool. A CV grows by accruing desirable competencies during an individual's professional life. A well nurtured CV enables a doctor to get the jobs he wants.

A shrewd doctor acquires professional competencies (communication, work ethic, clinical, qualifications, team working, clinical audit, clinical risk management, teaching, leadership and the essential non-clinical) as early in his career as possible. These competences are essential to the writing of a winning CV and success at interviews.

Increasingly requests for references tabulate attributes or skills– timekeeping, initiative, attitude to work, teamwork, clinical performance, dependability, communicating with patients and colleagues, sickness, etc– on which candidates is to be graded (poor, fair, satisfactory, good, outstanding, or similar categorisation).

Your competencies should increase over time to enable you to find better or more senior jobs. To ensure that your CV grows, you should:
• develop and sustain an appropriate work ethic
• perform the duties of a registered doctor effectively

Writing the medical CV

- develop effective professional communication skills
- contribute to team working willingly
- contribute to service leadership
- undertake clinical audit and research
- master effective education and teaching skills
- contribute to clinical risk management
- professional development
- personal development

6.2 Work ethic

Getting your first job is/was one of the hurdles on your way to building a career in medicine. Your CV may get you short-listed for the job you like. However to secure the post you need good references from your seniors or colleagues.

Attitude to work, self motivation, time management and initiative are important. Your technical expertise and work ethic enable your referees to confidently commend you for jobs. The GMC's *"Good Medical Practice"* asks:

Attitudes
Reliability and probity
Is this doctor dependable? Does he/she display honesty and integrity?
Does he/she always act in the best interests of patients?

Initiative
Does this doctor show an appropriate degree of initiative?

Timekeeping
Is this doctor punctual and reliable?
Does he/she contact the unit to warn of a problem?

An appropriate work ethic involves:
- Working conscientiously, effectively and efficiently
- Self-motivation/ initiative, seeking help as necessary

Writing the medical CV

- Relating well to patients, colleagues and other members of staff.

6.3 Duties of a doctor

Effective clinical performance is the foundation of a medical career. Your CV may get you an interview, but you need good references to secure the post. The GMC states in *Good Medical Practice:*

Duties of a doctor registered with the GMC

- *make the care of your patient your first concern;*
- *treat every patient politely and considerately;*
- *respect patients' dignity and privacy;*
- *listen to patients and respect their views;*
- *give patients information in a way they can understand;*
- *respect the rights of patients to be fully involved in decisions about their care;*
- *keep your professional knowledge and skills up to date;*
- *recognise the limits of your professional competence;*
- *be honest and trustworthy;*
- *respect and protect confidential information;*
- *make sure that your personal beliefs do not prejudice patient care;*
- *act quickly to protect patients from risk if you have good reason to believe that you or a colleague may not be fit to practise;*
- *avoid abusing your position as a doctor; and*
- *work with colleagues in ways that best serve patients' interests.*

6.4 Effective communication

We send out CVs, completed application forms and application letters for recruiters to judge our suitability for posts. Our suitability is judged on the content, organisation and language of those documents.

To ensure good references, and to increase chances of success at interviews, an astute doctor will cultivate effective communications skills (speech and body language, active listening, and effective writing) and clinical competence. *Good Medical Practice* asks:

Communication skills

Does this doctor give the patient the information he/she asks for or needs about her/his condition, its treatment and prognosis, in a way the patient can understand?

Does he/she communicate adequately with colleagues and other health care professionals?

A wise doctor, whose first language is not English, strives to improve his writing skills and fluency in speaking the global business and professional language.

6.5 Teams and teamwork

Doctors "treat" patients through teams of professionals and support staff. A doctor's ability to collaborate with others strongly influences the course of his career and rewards. You ability to relate to patients (communication skills, courtesy and politeness) and colleagues (courtesy, amiability and team work) has an impact on your references.

Good Medical Practice asks questions a doctor's ability to work with others:

Working with other doctors
- *Is this doctor accessible?*
- *Does he/she work constructively as part of the clinical team?*
- *Does he/she respect the skills and contributions of others?*

Working with other health care professionals
- *Is this doctor accessible?*
- *Does he/she respect the skills and contributions of other health care workers?*
- *Does he/she delegate, consult and refer appropriately?*

The way a doctor relates to other health workers (nurses, doctors, therapists, technicians, ward clerks, managers, etc) colours the way her/his contribution is perceived. Interpersonal skills strongly influence the outcome of your career.

Prospective employers want to know if the doctor works well with other health care workers. Your referees will confidentially communicate their judgment of your team working skills to recruiters.

But who was responsible?

In the NHS, much is written and spoken about teams and team-working. However when something goes wrong there is a frantic search for an individual (a consultant or a chief executive) to blame. So contribute your best to teams.

6.6 Leadership skills

Senior doctors are expected to contribute to the administration (management) of their services. You should learn to manage (administer) yourself and to lead teams as early in your career as possible. *Good Medical Practice* asks:

Administration
- *Is this doctor efficient in the management of his/her own time and professional activities?*
- *Can he/she be relied upon to deal with the tasks required?*

Management is the art of doing things right (properly), while **leadership** is the ability to identify the right things to do. Management and leadership skills improve with good practice. Some people are good at management while others excel as leaders. Some are both good leaders and good managers.

Unfortunately, the NHS does not facilitate effective leadership training for hospital specialist registrars until they are appointed consultant– acquire management roles. Up to 60 % of SpRs (in 2003) do not feel confident enough to seek consultant posts six months after officially completing specialist training. The NHS has therefore, established a *New Consultant Entry Scheme* to equip former SpRs with management skills. How could so many specialist doctors fail to acquire management skills despite 4 to 5 years of compulsory RITA (Record of In-Training Assessment)? Was management education excluded from the curriculum?

The BMJ publishes articles on management– over 30 in "Tips" series alone. The NHS leadership website www.nhsleadershipqualities.nhs.uk hosts material on leadership.

Some doctors have acquired master of business administration (MBA) by distance learning at business schools (Bradford, Cranfield, Durham, Warwick, etc). The Financial Times (www.ft.com) publishes a ranking of MBA courses annually.

Entries found under *Leadership* in young doctors' CVs include:
- served as captain of school rugby football team
- was president of university medical students' association
- organise teaching programme for senior house officers
- serving as president of the junior doctors mess
- secretary of my village soccer football club.

6.7 Clinical audit

Doctors are expected to evaluate their clinical performance. The Department of Health and the Commission for Health Improvement and Audit take clinical audit as evidence of good medical practice.

Present your audits at meetings and try to publish some. Abstracts of clinical audits enhance the quality of a CV. A published paper is impressive on an application form and in a CV.

6.8 Teaching

Teaching is the ability to communicate messages and demonstrate skills to other interested people. Doctors are expected to teach *students* and patients. They become complete *'doctors'* when they learn to teach effectively. *'Doctor'* means teacher, learned person, instructor on a specialised branch of knowledge. The GMC's *Good Medical Practice*[1] asks:

Teaching and training
* *Does this doctor accept responsibility for teaching junior colleagues?*
* *Is he/she honest and objective in assessing the performance of others?*
* *Does he/she ensure that juniors are properly supervised?*

In your CV you would list those activities in which you teach or supervise somebody in basic knowledge and/or practical skills:
* taught clinical medicine to medical students and house officers
* supervise new senior house officers in neonatal resuscitation
* tutor in emergency medicine and trauma for new doctors.

6.9 Clinical risk management

Health care risk is the likelihood of a patient suffering harm from clinical activity. The risk may be clinical (wrong diagnosis, wrong treatment, faulty equipment, etc), environmental (slippery floors, falling objects, etc.), or organisational (poor supplies, inadequate staff, etc). Risks are minimised by recognition and prevention.

Clinical governance aims to insure that the patient gets effective and safe treatment. An astute doctor appreciates the importance of clinical governance and risk management, the use of clinical guidelines and her role in the mission. She learns to describe her contribution to clinical governance in her CV and at interviews.

Research

Most hospital clinicians do not expect and should not be asked to do elaborate medical research. However they can join collaborative clinical studies.

Including audits and research in your CV

In a junior doctor's CV, research and audit can be described under *"research and audit"*. As your career grows and you accumulate audits and research studies, you need separate headings.

A brief summary of the audit, similar to the *'Abstract'* of a published paper, but shorter, should be entered under *'Audit'* in your CV.

RSV status in babies with bronchiolitis admitted for intensive care.
Catsford Infirmary, Dec. 2000 to Feb. 2001.

Case notes of 57 babies discharged from the paediatric intensive care unit over three winter months with a diagnosis of bronchiolitis were analysed.

Collection of naso-paharyngeal aspirates for RSV was recorded in 47 (82%). A result of the RSV test was found in 43/57 (75%), and a positive RSV test in 39 (83%) of tests.

All samples for RSV testing and the result should be recorded in case notes. The audit should be repeated in a future bronchiolitis season.

Please note the amount of detail in the summary. It gives answers to *"what, where, when* and *how"* of the audit: *what* was done, *where* it was done, *when* it was done, *how* it was done, *what* was found and *what* should be done next.

Publishing clinical audits

Good audits are publishable. Journals dedicated to clinical audit exist. If two doctors of otherwise equal qualifications and experience apply for a post, the applicant with publications to her name is likely to be preferred. Yes, that may be unfair. The doctor with no publications may be a better clinician. But how do potential employers know? There is bias in favour of the published doctor. So start early and get published.

Getting published takes time (developing ideas, doing the audit or research, analysing the data, writing the paper and finding a journal that will publish it). It is not something you do the weekend before sending off your CV in response to an advert on www.bmj.com

6.10 Professional development

Certificates of attendance at courses, seminars and workshops should be kept as evidence of continuing professional development. Any activity that makes you a better clinician, better leader or more effective counts as *continuous professional development*.

Courses attended

Two weeks in every 6 months (junior doctors) should be spent on study leave– attending a course, preparing for or taking membership exams, learning new skills or other activity relevant to your career.

Choose your courses carefully. Cardiopulmonary resuscitation and life support courses (ALS, ASLS, APLS, etc), are becoming desirable and could become essential for short listing for SHO and SpR jobs. That is, if somebody has done them and your have not, he would be preferred.

Presentations

Present your audit and research studies at local, and external meetings whenever possible. Keep a record of your presentations and quote them as appropriate in your CV. Example:

> **Cat scratch fever.** *Weekly medical grand round.*
> *Catsford Infirmary, Catsford, 16 Oct. 2003.*

An HO, SHO or registrar may include departmental, and hospital external presentations in the CV. However, lists of courses and presentations are not impressive in a senior doctor's CV.

Senior doctors are expected to show evidence of leadership and managerial achievements. A record of presentations and courses attended would be reserved for the annual appraisal interview.

6.11 Personal development

There are many non-clinical skills that enhance a doctor's attraction to clinical teams and hence employability. These include:

Information technology (typing, graphics, website design and desktop publishing). Clinical units would welcome help in designing and producing patient education booklets and pamphlets.

Writing skills are useful in developing, editing and producing patient education / information booklets and leaflets. Some clinical teams and individual doctors have written and had published books.

Language(s) are useful in multilingual Britain. Sometimes patients do not receive full services until an interpreter has been found.

Summary

- *Perform clinical duties effectively*: Effective clinical performance is the foundation of a medical career.

- *Have an effective work ethic*– self motivation, time management and initiative are important.

- *Learn to manage (administer) your service*– Acquire management and leadership skills (in small doses!).

- *Learn to work on teams* and appreciate the roles of other professionals. Interpersonal skills strongly influence the outcome of your career.

- **Develop effective communication skills** (speech, body language, writing) are essential to career advancement. Send your best CV and cover letters to recruiters. Learn to speak and behave in a was that advances your career.

- **'Doctor' means teacher**, learned person, instructor on a specialised branch of knowledge. Teaching is the ability to communicate ideas or practical skills to other interested people. Doctors become complete *'doctors'* when they learn to teach effectively.

- **Clinical audit** is the comparison of clinical performance to a standard- they way it should have been done. It is one of the signs of growth in the CV and hence the clinician.

- **Clinical governance** means insuring that the patient gets effective clinical care and is not hurt by the clinical activity or the environment.

- **Manage clinical risk involves** recognition and prevention of the likelihood a patient suffering harm as a result of a clinical action or lack of it. Health care risks may be clinical, environmental or organisational.

- **Acquire essential qualifications and skills** complete membership and attend appropriate cardiopulmonary resuscitation and life support courses (ALS, ASLS, APLS, etc) as soon as possible– they are highly desirable for all clinicians in acute medicine.

- **Mastering non-medical skills** like *IT skills* (typing, desktop publishing, etc), *writing skills* and *languages* can improve a doctor's employability.

References

1. GMC. **Good medical practice**. 3rd edition. London: GMC 2001

Writing the medical CV

2. **Shorter Oxford English Dictionary.** Oxford: Oxford University Press 2002.

3. Loeb M, Kindel S. **Leadership for Dummies.** New York: Wiley 1999.

4. Houghton A, Peters T, Bolton J. **What do new consultants have to say?** BMJ 2002; 325:s145.

5. **The New Consultant Entry Scheme.** BMJ 2004; 328:s39.

6. Griffiths M. **Tips on...Report writing.** BMJ Careers 2004; 328:s28.

7. Dash P. **Tips on...Developing a strategy.** BMJ 2002; 324:s207

7 Clinical documents

Clinical documents

7.1 Need for clinical documents

Clinical documents record (document) clinical events in notes, letters or reports so that they can be consulted later or used to pass on information to individuals and/or organisations.

Letters convey or seek information. Reports communicate the findings of some study/investigation to the body that commissioned them or the general public.

7.2 Legal status of clinical documents

Clinical notes, letters and reports belong to the Secretary of State for Health (government). They acquire legal status as soon as they are made. Patients have a legal right to see their notes and to receive copies, including X-rays and scans.

7.3 Preparing clinical documents

Clinical documents are usually typed (word-processed) by medical secretaries. The secretary types the document from a tape recorded by the clinician, a hand written script and rarely from dictated notes.

7.3.1 Organising the content

Think out what you want to include and exclude from the letter or report. Use subheadings to structure the material. These may be included in the dictation or script and the typed document. Even if you do not want subheadings in the finished document you should organise the content along the same framework (see examples below).

7.3.2 Using a tape recorder

It is your duty to speak clearly so that the secretary can make out your words. Indicate where new paragraphs and essential punctuation marks should go, particularly brackets [{( )}], comma (,), dash (–), and the full stop or period (.).

Spell out unusual words. Name individuals and organisations you want to receive copies of the document.

Indicate how you want your name to appear on the document, which degree(s) to quote and the attribution– Registrar to Mr Dorset, consultant surgeon, etc.

7.3.3 Writing the hand script

Write so that the secretary can make out the words. Organise the contents under 'headings' even if you do not write them down.

Write your name, degrees and attributions the way you want them on the typed document. List individuals and organisations you wish to receive copies.

7.4 Signing documents

Signing documents means more than scribbling your signature in the proper place. It is your duty, before you sign the document, to ensure that it says what you wanted to say, not less and not more. *Good medical Practice* states:

Writing reports, giving evidence and signing documents
51. You must be honest and trustworthy when writing reports, completing or signing forms, or providing evidence in litigation or other formal inquiries.

This means that you must take reasonable steps to verify any statement before you sign a document. You must not write or sign documents which are false or misleading because they omit relevant information. If you have agreed to prepare a report, complete or sign a document or provide evidence, you must do so without unreasonable delay.

Writing the medical CV

You are legally responsible for its content. It goes out under your name.

Therefore:
* Read the typed document carefully and check for errors of content, spelling, grammar and meaning, drugs (names, preparations, doses, frequency, etc.)

* Is the message expressed the way you wanted to express it? This is important in medico-legal issues. Lawyers love *discovering* meaning in unguarded expressions.

* Make appropriate corrections and get the document retyped. Next time prepare the manuscript or dictation more carefully. If the mistakes were your doing, apologise to the secretary.

* Only sign documents whose content you are happy with.

* Only an identical copy of the document signed by the author should be kept (in patient's notes or other appropriate place).

7.5 Essence of clinical note making
When you make entries into patient notes or write a clinical letter, take care:
* think of what you are going to write and how you will phrase it
* write politely; there is no need to record your rudeness
* avoid ambiguity, your notes should be clear
* use simple, short words; short sentences and short paragraphs
* avoid superfluous words and phrases.

While making notes:
* Ensure the patient's names and record number are on the page
* Start by writing down the date and time
* Write on all lines– no empty lines between script
* Record current medications, dosage, delivery method, devices
* Record consent from, advice to, discussion with patients/parents

- Enter laboratory results into body of notes as soon as you get them
- Record clinical progress, procedures and treatments daily, and whenever there is a change in condition or clinical action
- Record unusual incidents; discuss them with senior doctor/sister
- Record future plans: 'Follow up' [when, whom…], 'No Follow up'
- Record the date and time of discharge
- Sign and print your name after every entry.

7.6 Clinical letters

The aim of a clinical letter is to convey information or seek advice (consultation) or practical assistance (referral).

The content of the letter varies depending on the condition, severity and course of the condition and the recipient. Details depend on when, in the course of clinical contact, the letter is written. Initial letters tend to be longer than subsequent ones.

7.6.1 Identification

Clinical letters quote references to identify the patient (hospital number) and initials of the writer and the secretary who typed the letter.

7.5.2 Date of writing
7.5.3 Recipient's name and address
7.5.4 Patient's name (date of birth) and address

7.6.2 Clinical problem or diagnosis

If the diagnosis is known you should state it here. If a diagnosis has not been made the clinical problem(s) should be stated.

A patient is seen with chronic abdominal pain and bloody diarrhoea. The first clinic letter might say:

  Problem: Abdominal pain and bloody diarrhoea.

Following investigations a diagnosis of 'Ulcerative colitis' was made. Subsequent letters about the same subject would say:

Diagnosis: Ulcerative colitis.

If complications or problems develop, they should be added to the diagnosis:

Diagnosis: Ulcerative colitis, with arthropathy, anterior uveitis, etc.

7.6.3 Medication/ therapy

All treatments (drugs: dosage, preparation, route/devices, frequency, duration, etc.) should be stated, as they would appear on a prescription. This will enable any doctor (GP or in hospital) to review treatment with the patient, and if necessary make changes. It is impossible to recommend changes if you are not sure of the dosage or its frequency.

> *"**Becotide 2 puffs b.d**" was recorded in the notes and letter to the GP. How much Becotide was that: 100mcg, 200mcg, 400mcg or 800mcg?*

Physical treatments (physiotherapy, occupational therapy, etc) should also be included in the clinic or discharge letter.

7.6.4 History

Essential elements of the history (symptoms, duration, investigations and their results, past treatments and their effects) and patient's concerns should be communicated.

7.6.5 Examination

Both positive and significant negative (absent) signs should be included in this section. Their interpretation should be given.

7.6.6 Investigations

Known results and their interpretation should be communicated. Planned investigations should be stated.

7.6.7 Recommendations and advice

Recommendations and advice given to the patient should be described:

"eat less and exercise more" *(hypertensive, overweight)*

"continue thyroxine for life" *(patient with hypothyroidism)*

7.6.8 Follow-up

Arrangements for 'follow-up' (future clinic visits) should also be reported. E.g.:

 – *Review every 3 months– check weight, BP and HbA1c*

 – *Continue using splint for 6 weeks*

 – *Discharged*

7.7 Examples of clinical letters

7.7.1. Hospital discharge summary

7.7.2. Outpatient clinic letter

7.7.3. Primary care referral to hospital

7.7.4. Primary care referral to hospital

7.7.5. Intra-hospital referral

7.7.6. Letter to a parent

7.9.1. A report for a solicitor.

7.7.1. Hospital discharge summary

Brambleton Infirmary
Gladstone Street
Brambleton BZ75 9FT

Our Ref: X4534652

29 June 2001

Dr J Williams
Moss Lane Surgery
Duke Way
Brambleton BZ76 3EF

Dear Dr Williams

Re: Donald McDonald (born 12. 04. 2001)
45 Nottingham Close, Brambleton BZ76 8QL.

Admitted: 21.06.2001. **Discharged:** 27.06.2001.
Consultant: Dr M Gregory

Diagnoses: Grade 4 Vesico-Ureteric Reflux on Left
E.coli Urinary Tract Infection

Prophylaxis: Trimethoprim 2mg/kg at night (now 10 mg)

History: Donald was off feeds and feverish for 2 days. Trimethoprim had been stopped. His parents said he was well and did not needed antibiotics.

Examination: He was miserable, febrile 39°C.

Investigations: A clean catch urine sample had few red blood cells and >100 WBC. E.coli cultured from his urine was sensitive to cephalexin and trimethoprim.

Treatment: Donald received intravenous cephalexin for 5 days.

Advice: UTI antibiotic prophylaxis was discussed with his parents. The dose of trimethoprim should be adjusted monthly. His parents were given a leaflet on UTI.

Follow-up: Donald will be seen in Dr Gregory's clinic in 8 weeks.

Yours sincerely

VSatish

Dr.V.Satish MRCP
Registrar to Dr M Gregory.

Dr Satish's letter to Dr Williams, the patient's GP, clearly:
- identifies the patient by record number, name, age and address
- states when the child was admitted and discharged
- names the child's consultant, to whom inquiries may be directed
- gives the reason for hospitalisation (E.coli UTI in Grade 4 left VUR)
- highlights home management (drug, dose regimen and current dose)
- briefly describes the history (off feeds, feverish), physical findings (fever), investigations (urinalysis, urine culture and sensitivity),
- states hospital management (IV cephalexin for 5 days)
- states advice given (UTI prophylaxis with trimethoprim discussed; monthly dose adjustment; parents given leaflet on UTI)
- states future plans (Follow-up in Dr Gregory's clinic in 8 weeks).

7.7.2. Outpatient clinic letter

Brambleton Infirmary
Gladstone Street
Brambleton BZ75 9FT

Our Ref Z0486873

29 July 2002

Dr J Williams
Moss Surgery
Moss Lane
Brambleton BZ76 4ZP

Dear Dr Williams

Re: Jennifer Leighton (born 12.04.1986)
      23 Magellan Drive, Brambleton BZ76 8DL.

Problem: Convulsions while working on a computer

Investigations: EEG, CT head

I saw Jennifer with her mother in Dr Hertz's clinic. Jennifer felt fuzzy while working on computer at school, 18 days ago. She woke to find herself on the classroom floor. Her teacher said Jennifer fell off a chair, had jerking arms and legs for about 10 minutes; slept for 20 minutes and was drowsy for a while afterwards.

Jennifer had a brief fit while working on computer at home about three months back. She has no history of fits or chronic headaches. Her school work is excellent. A twin sister is treated for photosensitive epilepsy.

Her weight and height are on the 75th centile. Her BP was 120/65 mmHg, the skin, cranial nerves, optic fundi and reflexes were normal.

Dr Hertz saw Jennifer and said she might have photosensitive epilepsy like her twin sister. Anticonvulsant treatment was discussed with Jennifer and her mother. It was agreed to wait for the EEG report before considering anticonvulsant therapy.

Writing the medical CV

Jennifer's should only use computers with non-glare, non-flicker monitors in a well lighted rooms. She should sit at least 6 feet from the TV set and should avoid flickering lights and Discos.

Jennifer will be reviewed in 6 weeks time

Yours sincerely

JBates

John Bates MRCPCH

SpR to Dr Hertz

Dr Bates has written a letter that:

- identifies the patient by hospital number, names and address

- highlights the problem (convulsions while working on a computer), and names investigation planned (EEG, CT head)

- summarises the history (convulsion while working on computer, witnessed by her teacher. One previous fits; twin sister has photosensitive epilepsy)

- states results of physical exam (growth, BP and CNS), and the suspected diagnosis (photosensitive epilepsy like her twin)

- records discussion (mother agreed to wait for EEG report before decision on anticonvulsants; use non-glare computers monitors; sit 6 feet from TV, avoid flickering lights and Discos)

- states follow-up plans (Jennifer will be reviewed in 6 weeks time).

7.7.3. Primary care referral to hospital

Jubilee Surgery
Duke Way,
Brambleton BZ76 3EF

23 June 2002

Dr Mark Gregory
Consultant Paediatrician
Brambleton Infirmary
Gladstone Street
Brambleton BZ75 9FT

Dear Dr Gregory

Re: Imran Mohamed Khalifar (d.o.b 23-5- 1998)
34 Duke Way, Brambleton BZ76 3EF

Please see this lad who has had a cough for 3 years. He is not responding to
asthma inhalers. I had to give him oral steroid recently. His mother brought him back
saying her son's cough was much better after oral steroids given 2 weeks ago.

Yours sincerely

M Bramble

Mary Bramble
GP registrar to Dr K. Shah

Dr Shah discussed the letter with his registrar. He said the suspected diagnosis
and current treatment were not included; that the letter implied that the child
was receiving regular oral steroids. How inhalers were used in a 3 year was not
stated. It was not clear what advice Dr Bramble was seeking. She rewrote letter
that afternoon.

7.7.4. Primary care referral to hospital

Jubilee Surgery
Duke Way,
Brambleton BZ76 3EF

25 June 2002

Dr Mark Gregory
Consultant Paediatrician
Brambleton Infirmary
Gladstone Street
Brambleton BZ75 9FT

Dear Dr Gregory

Re: Imran Mohamed Khalifar (d.o.b 23. 5. 1999)
   34 Duke Way, Brambleton BZ76 3EF

Would you see Imran, a 3 year old with a chronic cough and advise. He is not responding to Ventolin inhalers 2 puffs via Volumatic for asthma.

Two weeks ago he was given oral prednisolone 10mg for 3 days because his cough was worse and he wheezed.

He was back yesterday with cough and wheeze worse on exercise. His mother said the asthma was much better after the oral steroids.

Imran's father and uncle use Becotide inhalers for asthma. Is it safe to give a 3 year old long term inhaled steroids?

Yours sincerely

MBramble
Mary Bramble
GP registrar to Dr K. Shah

7.7.5. Intra-hospital referral

Brambleton Infirmary
Gladstone Street
Brambleton BZ75 9FT

Our Ref Z0486579

23 June 2002

Mr Robert Staples
Consultant Surgeon
Brambleton Infirmary
Brambleton BZ75 9FT.

Dear Robert

Re: Thomas MacAfee (born 12.07.1991)
    56 Lanten Close, Brambleton BZ76 9QL.

Problem: Enlarged (5 cm) firm lymph node mass in neck.
Request: Evaluation with a view to an excision biopsy.

Thomas has a 5cm diameter lymph node on the left side of his neck. The gland was noted 6 weeks ago and is getting bigger. He has night fevers and has lost 2 kg in weight in the last 4 weeks.

A sister had tuberculosis 5 years ago. Thomas' chest X-ray is normal; and two tuberculin tests are negative. Is Thomas' gland infective or neoplastic?

Regards,

M Gregory
Dr Mark Gregory MD FRCPCH
Consultant Paediatrician.

cc. Dr Kamran Shah, Jubilee Surgery, Duke Way, Brambleton BZ76 3EF

7.7.6 Letter to a parent

Brambleton Infirmary
Gladstone Street
Brambleton BZ75 9FT

Our Ref: X4534652

23 May 2002

Mrs Fiona McDonald
45 Nottingham Close
Brambleton BZ76 8QL.

Dear Mrs McDonald

Re: Tests to sort out Daniel's kidney problem

This is to inform you that the scan of Donald's kidneys shows that the left ureter (a tube taking urine from the kidney to the bladder) is still dilated.

We need to find out why this is so. I have asked Dr Peters, a consultant radiologist at this hospital, to do some special scans of Donald's urinary system.

Could we meet in my clinic on Wednesday 5th June 2002 at 11 a.m. to discuss the ultrasound scan report and the additional tests?

Please continue with trimethoprim at night to prevent a water infection.

Yours sincerely

M Gregory
Dr Mark Gregory MD FRCPCH
Consultant Paediatrician

cc: Dr J Williams, Moss Surgery, Moss Lane, Brambleton BZ 76 4ZP

Letters to patients or parents are more difficult to write well. Medical information has to be conveyed accurately without jargon. They are usually sometimes longer than those to the GP on the same problem.

7.8. Clinical Reports

Commissioned reports have terms of reference– the nature of the investigation (area of concern/interest), its scope and limitations. These govern the detail of the report and its recommendations.

7.8.1 What is a clinical report?

A clinical report is a document written to communicate clinical findings and recommendations about a clinical problem, incident or phenomenon to a person or persons with a legitimate interest in the subject.

Before writing a report you should have a clear understanding of:
• the purpose of the report
• the audience (who it is aimed at)
• who will read it, and who will use it
• what you want to communicate, achieve, how and why?

Think about the audience. What is their:
• authority (ability to act on the report)?
• knowledge of the subject (*to judge the pitch of the report*)?
• level of education (*to decide appropriate language*)?
• attitude towards the subject (*biases to overcome*)?

The majority of clinical reports (clinical audits, hospital incidents and case reports for police or social services) are relatively easy to write. However when responding to a complaint about clinical care, the report must be written much more deliberately. Your report could be used in legal proceedings against you and your health care organisation (hospital trust or PCT).

7.8.2 Structure of a report

A report has a structure– a beginning, a body and an end:
- an introduction to say what the report is about
- the body to tell readers what you want them to know
- a summary to state the essence of the report.

Published reports have a standard structure– what readers expect to find when they open a *report*. If your report departs too far from this structure, the unusual format may reduce the impact of your findings and recommendations.

Some reports are so brief that the usual structure is condensed. However you should write them with headings in mind.

A long report is organised in sections: title page, contents list, summary, an introduction, body of the report, conclusions, recommendations, references (bibliography) and appendices.

Title page shows:
– the title (official name of the report)
– the author(s') name(s)
– a statement of the subject of the report
– the date (of writing or publication).

The Contents list shows the sections or chapters in the report (including appendices, references, etc) and the pages on which they start.

The Summary should outline the report in two or three short paragraphs. Summaries are written last, in the third person singular.

"This report considered the use of herbal remedies in infertility...."

The **Introduction** gives a concise explanation of the terms (aims/ context) of the inquiry. It should contain brief background information to enable the reader to understand the subject of inquiry, its findings and recommendations.

The body of the report is where you write the findings of the inquiry. It should:
– be based on an analysis of issues and findings
– supported by evidence and argument
– clearly distinguish between fact and opinion.

The body should be subdivided into sections (or chapters) if the report is long. Sections should be sequentially numbered *(as in this book)* to assist reference to material. Graphs and charts should be used where and when appropriate.

Conclusions are the judgements (opinions) you have reached after studying the subject:

> *"The high mortality were caused by shortage of antibiotics and not poor clinical skills or lack of effort."*

Conclusions should not be confused with recommendations.

Recommendations are the actions your conclusions lead you to believe are necessary to improve the situation:

> *"All new midwives and paediatric staff should be taught neonatal resuscitation."*

The *references* (bibliography) section gives details of sources cited in the report. Use the Vancouver format: *"Uniform Requirements for manuscripts submitted to Biomedical Journals" in* citing references. Example:

1. International Committee of Medical Journal Editors. **Uniform Requirements for manuscripts submitted to Biomedical Journals.** *Ann Inter Med* 1997; 126: 36-47.

2. Jain A, Ogden J. **General practitioners' experiences of patients' complaints: qualitative study.** *BMJ* 1999; 318:1596-1599

Appendices

This is the place where information not essential to the flow of the argument of the report, but which some readers may wish to study, is placed.

7.9 Reports with legal potential

You will, in your medical career, be asked (instructed) by lawyers to write medico-legal reports on patients you have seen. A & E doctors are frequently asked to write reports and give evidence in court on patients they have treated. Paediatric registrars are encouraged to write reports (under supervision) on children they have examined for suspected non-accidental (inflicted) injury.

When writing medico-legal reports (for social services, police and lawyers) remember that your report may be used in a court of law and you may be cross-examine on its contents. So:

- State your names, qualification and appointment and in which capacity you saw the patient.

- Explain why you are an expert in the field. Do not claim an expertise you do not have. Don't let your emotions affect the tone of your report. Do not include anything that you would not repeat under oath.

- The report will be read by people with little medical knowledge. Use short words, short phrases and short paragraphs. Explain unavoidable medical jargon. Describe events sequentially to produce clear and logical document.

- List all sources of the evidence you used to reach your diagnosis and conclusions, however insignificant or trivial it may seem. List documents you read or used, telephone conversations, and face to face interviews (give names of people you talked to in your evaluation of the case).

- List the investigations you used to obtain information and to a make the diagnosis [(history, physical examination, measurements of lesions (bruises, abrasions, lacerations, tears, fractures, etc,) laboratory tests, X-rays and

7.9.1. A report for a solicitor

Department of Orthopaedics
Brambleton Infirmary
Gladstone Street
Brambleton BZ75 9FT

Our Ref: Z0686983

23 July 2003

Mr Kate Rumple
Nightingale and Swift Solicitors
Rumple Avenue
Catsford CZ15 2GF.

Dear Miss Rumple

Re: Simon Redwood of 12 Duke Way, Catsford M75 2JF.

Subject: Fracture of right femur

I, Kevin Moynihan, MB ChB FRCS, employed as consultant orthopaedic surgeon at Catsford Infirmary, examined Mr Redwood in the Emergency Room of the hospital at 10 a.m. on 21 July 2002. He said he had been injured in a road traffic accident..

There was an oval skin bruise of about 5 cm in diameter at about 15 cm above the right knee. The right femur (thigh bone) had a complete break under the bruise. The skin was not broken.

The fracture was aligned and fixed with a metal rod inserted into the femur. He was discharged home two days later. He will need to use a crutch for 6 weeks to avoid putting weight onto his right leg.

Mr Redwood will be followed in my clinic at this hospital. Full recovery is expected.

Yours sincerely

K Moynihan
Kevin Moynihan MB ChB FRCS
Consultant Orthopaedic Surgeon

scans, photographs (essential in skin bruises, tears, swellings, etc.)].

• Separate facts from their interpretation. Keep fact separate from opinion. Separate interpretation from conclusions.

• Summarise your findings and opinion and place it at the beginning of the report.

• Number the pages and use the patient's name as a 'footer'. If the report is long, include a title page, a contents list and a summary.

• Sign and date the report.

Example
The lawyer representing a passenger in one of the vehicles involved in the accident has asked the orthopaedic surgeon for a report on the injuries, their treatment and prognosis *(page 152)*.

7.10 Responding to complaints
Letters of complaint are usually addressed to the chief executive officer (CEO) of trusts. Patients may however write to any senior member of the trust (chairman, board directors, a senior doctor or nurse, a senior therapist or a manager). Such complaints are processed through one office (the complaints office or the public relations office).

7.10.1 Processing written complains
Usually:
• the CEO requests the Public Relations Officer (PRO) to handle the complaint (*contact named individual(s) and others and get their response*)

• the PRO writes to individual(s) cited in the complaint to describe on their involvement in the case/incident.

• the individual(s) cited respond in writing to the PRO (*present their views on*

Writing the medical CV

the allegations made in the complaint)

- the PRO may seek comments from other individuals present at the incident to clarify issues (*other persons may have witnessed or been involved in the incident from which the complaint arose*)

- the PRO drafts a letter (for the CEO) replying to the complaint (*chief executives do not have the time to investigate and respond personally)*

- *it is good practice for PRO to show the draft response to the doctor complained about. If the doctor disagrees then they can discuss the draft*).

- the CEO reads the draft letter and if it is satisfactory, signs it. The official response is then sent to the complainant.

Most complainants are satisfied by the chief executive's reply. However some are not and may contact their MP or consult lawyers to sue the trust and doctor.

7.10.2 Preparing a response

Before writing your response, carefully read the complaint again. What is the complaint about? Try and recall the incident leading to the complaint. Make notes of your recollections. Discuss the complaint with you consultant or an informed and trusted colleague (if you are a consultant) or better still with the MDU or MPS.

Respond only to issues raised in the complaint. Do not open new topics. Do not mention difficulties you might have had with the patient in the past. You should respond to all issues raised in the complaint– and nothing more.

If matters seem serious, consult your medical protection organisation (MDU, MPS or other) immediately and inform the trust's legal unit. Do not alter– erase, remove or add to, or otherwise change the patient's notes. Experts can tell if you do. Speak to your consultant; or discuss the problem with a trusted friend (if you are a consultant).

7.11 Handling press interest

If the press get involved, **do not discuss the case with reporters** (TV, radio, newspaper or any other reporter)– **not even off record**. Nothing is off record for a reporter.

Patient Confidentiality: *Protecting and Providing Information* includes:

Protecting information

2. *When you are responsible for personal information about patients you must make sure that it is effectively protected against improper disclosure at all times.*

3. *Many improper disclosures are unintentional. You should not discuss patients where you can be overheard or leave patients' records, either on patients where you can be overheard or leave patient records, either on paper or screen, where they can be seen by other patients, unauthorised health care staff or the public.*

Whenever possible you should take steps to ensure that steps to ensure your consultations with patients are private.

The complainant has the freedom to talk to the press. You do not. Maintain patient confidentiality. Leave communicating with the press to the trust's public relations office.

Summary

- Clinical notes and letters are legal documents with legal implications. They legally belong to the Secretary of State for Health. The patient has a legal right to see her notes and to receive copies.

- Every entry into case notes should have the dated and time of writing. The writer should sign and printed her/his name.

- The record or message should be clear, concise and as simple as possible using short words, short phrase and short paragraphs.

- Clinical documents record clinical activity or event in notes so that they can be consulted later or used to pass on information.

- The aim of a clinical letter is to transmit or seek information or advice (consultation) or practical assistance (referral).

- The letter must identify the patient, state clinical problems/diagnosis, treatment and planned action

- A clinical report communicates clinical findings about a clinical problem, incident or phenomenon to people with a legitimate interest in the subject and may recommend a remedy or action.

- A report has a standard structure. An unusual format may reduce the impact of the findings and/or recommendations.

- When writing medico-legal reports:
– keep as objective as possible
– do not claim an expertise you do not have
– separate facts from their interpretation
– separate interpretation from conclusions
– distinguish the probable from the possible, and
– cite sources of evidence for your conclusions.
- Only sign documents whose content you are happy with.

- If a patient complains about you, seek advice from your consultant, or senior colleague. Do not alter or add to patient case record.

- If matters are serious consult your medical protection organisation (MDU, MPS or other) right away.

- Do not discuss clinical complaints with the press- not even off record. Maintain patient confidentiality.

Further Reading

1. GMC. **Confidentiality: Protecting and Providing Information**. Sept. 2000.

2. Mort S. **Professional Report Writing.** London: Cower 1995.

3. Suresh K. **Writing a medico-legal report.** *BMJ* 2002; 325: s111

4. Griffiths M. *Tips on....* **Report writing.** BMJ 2004;328: s28.

---

8. Clinical Audit

Clinical Audit

8.1 What is clinical audit?

To **audit** means to account for, to balance, check, examine, to verify something against expectations, against what should have been done.

Clinical audit = checking that a clinical activity went as planned, was done as expected. Clinical activities (performance, outcome, etc) are scrutinized or compared with expectations, with standards.

[*Standard* = level, degree, benchmark, specification, guide....].

Clinical audit is not research. It is easy to confuse clinical *audit* with *research.* Similar tools are used in both endeavours, but clinical audit is not synonymous with clinical research.

In clinical audit what should be done, how, when the expected performance are known or assumed. A standard is used to measure performance. The auditor checks to see if performance met the standard.

Research (re-search) means *searching again* for an insight, an answer to a question or problem. The researcher must find answers to *what, how, when, why, who/whom* of the problem/question. Unlike audit, the researcher does not know the right answer.

Good clinical audits may unearth important questions. Why is performance so good/poor? Why are guidelines not followed? Such questions may be pursued by research.

8.2 Who needs clinical audit?

Clinical audit is beneficial to clinicians and the organisations (hospital, trust or clinic) they works in. Clinical audit:

* enables the individual or organisation to systematically examine their performance and/or outcomes against standards (e.g. guidelines)

* helps clinicians or the organisation to identify deficiencies in performance and resources, and provides evidence for what should be terminated, changed or encouraged (disseminated).

* facilitates the collection of evidence on which change in standards, practices and provision of resources may be based.

8.3 Audit standards

Clinical audit involves making judgments (satisfactory, better or worse). Judging requires comparison with acceptable practice, expected outcomes or norms. So standards or comparators are necessary. If they are not available they are set empirically (guessed initially) and adjusted with experience.

Where do clinical standards come from?

(**a**) *Performance at leading organisations* (hospitals) sets the standards for:
* *clinical issues*– diagnosis, treatment, survival, complication rates, etc.
* *managerial issues*– staffing needs, service costs, user rates, etc.

(**b**) *Published reports* of related research and audits in medical and health service management journals

(**c**) *Retrospective studies* have provided data for setting preliminary standards.

(**d**) *Pilot studies* may be necessary to try out new practices before the norm, the standards, can be gauged.

(**e**) *Monitoring current practice* and ironing out problems may lead to better outcomes. The new practices and outcomes then become standards against which future performance is judged.

8.4 Types of health care audit

- *Clinical decisions*: diagnosis, treatments, conformity to guidelines, prescribing habits, etc.

- *Clinical outcomes*: survival, re-admissions, complications) after some intervention.

- *Managerial targets*: waiting times, turnover, hospital stay, cost per unit of activity, productivity, waste (blood, drugs, disposables, etc.).

- *Complaints*: causes, response, resolution, complaint rates, etc.

8.5 Sources of information

Data for clinical audit can be gathered from many sources.
- *clinical notes* (paper and computer based)
- *pathology records* (tissue analysis- sampled in life or postmortem)
- *managerial records* (financial, absence record, staff turnover, etc.)
- *patient complaints* (causes, response, resolution, rates, etc.)
- *published data* (medical journals, internet, local service reports, trust reports, reports from/about peer organisations, etc.).

8.6 Requirements for clinical audit

Informative audits are not cheap. They require time, money, people and the will to do them well. Small audits are useful as training tools for novices, but should not be used to determine major changes in practice/policy.

An informative clinical audit needs:
- An intriguing / important problem to audit

- An intrigued / challenged mind to perform or supervise the audit
- Integrity/ skill in making judgments on disorganised data
- Resources (people, materials, money, time, space) for the audit.

8.7 Auditing a clinical issue

Novices underestimate the time and tedium involved in doing audits:

• culling information from case notes can be frustrating (missing notes, missing data, scattered reports, illegibility, notes wanted elsewhere).

• data from large organization may be difficult to obtain because of concerns about *security* and *confidentiality or* lack of urgency at the organisation.

• interviewing people is expensive in time and human resources (time from regular work or hiring assistants).

• *questionnaires* are *difficult to design* (for reliability and relevancy) and may not be completed by the *relevant subjects*.

Start early and get on with it.

8.8 Analysing audit data

Most audits do not require complicated statistical analysis. Simple tabulations and calculation of percentages is usually enough.

The importance of the difference between what was observed (happened) and what was expected (should have occurred) is determined by **quantitative** analysis or **statistical** analysis. This calculates the statistical **significance** *(the likelihood)* that the observed differences occurred by chance?

A neglected aspect of audit is **qualitative** analysis for the causes of good, superior or poor performance. **Why** are things this bad or so good? Most audits stress how much the performance differs from the expected, but not why.

Why is essential in **qualitative** analysis, for understanding the cause of what was observed. *Why* is the performance so poor, or so outstanding? The cause of the observed differences is essential to improving the activity. Without **why**, there is no **how** to guide improvements.

8.9 Writing the audit report

The subject is **introduced**, **methods** described, **results** revealed and discussed in relation to previous audits or studies in the area. The **discussion** should point out how the audit could have been done better.

Audit reports follow IMRD, the usual format for scientific papers. I MRD = Introduction, Methods, Results, and Discussion.

Conclusions based on the audit are drawn and *Recommendations* to correct identified flaws, maintain and disseminate the good performance are made. Recommendations should be sensible and practical.

Before it is released, the report should be given a *title* on a *title page*, a *summary*, a list of *contents*, a list of *references* and *appendices*.

8.9.1 Title page

The title page should display, in an attractive format:
- the title (the name of the report)
- names of author(s) and organisation(s)
- a statement on the subject of the report
- the date (of writing or publication).

The title should be short, pithy, embodying the essence of the audit. E.g.:
- Recording vital signs in acute asthma.
- Reduction in cancelled clinic appointments
- Hospital stay after hip replacement in the elderly
- Time to administration of streptokinase after heart attacks.

8.9.2 Summary

The summary should be succinct and encapsulate the findings of the audit. It is usually written after the body of the report is finished and placed in front of the report– after the title page. In official reports the summary is called an **executive summary**. Is it the only part of reports executives read?

8.9.3 Introduction

The introduction gives reasons for doing the audit. **Why** and **what** was done are explained. The current situation or practice is described to introduce the issue(s) to the reader.

8.9.4 Methods

Methods (methodology) describe *what* was done and *how* it was done.
• *What* did you do?
• *How* did you do it?

8.9.5 Results

What did you find? The results should be clearly described. Give enough detail (tables, graphs, quotes) to convey the results. State and describe the results only. Do not comment on their importance or meaning– that will be done in the discussion. If some material is long or complex, put it in an appendix.

8.9.6 Discussion

The discussion covers and attempts to answer, the following:
• What do the findings mean?
• How do they compare with previous audits?
• Could it have been done it better? How?

8.9.7 Conclusions

• What did you conclude from the audit?
• What are the implications of your audit?

8.9.8 Recommendations

Recommendations state what should be done to maintain (satisfactory situation), improve (unsatisfactory state) or disseminate (excellent) practice). A large, thorough audit may lead to closure of an unsatisfactory or service or policy.

Recommendations are followed by a brief comment about the need for and timing of a re-audit

8.9.9 References
The reference (bibliography) section lists all the sources quoted and the standards you have used.

8.10 Closing the audit loop
The recommendations of the audit may, if the authorities wish, be implemented and then re-audited. The *audit- reform- audit* is called **the audit loop** or **cycle** The loop (cycle) is closed after recommendations have been implemented, taken root and re-audited.

Summary
- *Clinical audit* = checking (judging) that past clinical activity went as expected, met standards

- Judgment requires comparison with standards or comparators

- Standard come from published reports, pilot projects, trial and error or empiricism (guess work)

- Good audits result from deployment of resources (time, money, people) and the will to do a good job

- Quantitative and qualitative audits analyses are essential to explaining the **magnitude** of the deference, **why** it exists and **how** to respond

- The audit report should be written under: Introduction, Methods, Results, Discussion, Conclusions and Recommendations

- Before it is released, the report is given a *title* on a *title page*, a *summary*, a list *contents*, a list of *references* ± *appendices*..

Further Reading

1. *Mort* S. **Professional Report Writing.** *Cower* 1995

2. NeLH Team. **Principles for Best Practice in Clinical Audit.** Radcliffe Medical Press Ltd 2002.

3. Griffiths M. *Tips on...* **Report writing.** BMJ 2004;328:s28.

9. Research and publish

Research and publish

9.1. What is research?

The word research has lost status. What should be basic reading is now called research. Some dictionaries suggest that *search* is more rigorous than *research!*

To me *research* (re-search) means *search again* for an insight, an answer, a solution, to an intriguing problem or question. It is more than reading relevant books, journals or searching the internet on the subject.

Accessible information should be gathered in order to clarify, to refine the question. Often the answer to what initially looked difficult is found in published texts or on the internet. To re-search you should have searched.

Semantics aside, why should you spend time and money to 'do' research?

9.2 Why 'do' research?

Not every SHO or registrar will do research or write theses for higher degrees. Research is discussed here to give you an idea of what is expected *if* and *when* the opportunity arises.

Good research is rewarding to the individual and society. The public benefits from research– telecommunications, engineering, physics, medicine (new diagnostics, pharmaceuticals, epidemiology, etc).

For most clinicians research involves looking for answers to clinical problems. Published authors are well regarded by their colleagues. They make presentations at meetings and publish articles in journals and chapters in learned books. They cite their publications in their CVs.

Doing research gives you the opportunity to learn the science of medical inquiry and the opportunity to enhance your CV.

9.3 Requirements for research

Research is not cheap. It requires:

- An intriguing/ important problem to solve
- Intelligence/ skill/ integrity in making judgments
- An intrigued/ challenged mind to perform or supervise the research
- Resources (people, materials, money, time, space, advice, support....).

9.3.1 Urge to research

Prerequisites for good research are an intriguing problem, and an interested (intrigued) and competent mind. Without the challenge it is difficult to sustain a research effort. The desire to solve a problem helps in finding time, space and the money for research.

9.3.2 Money for research

Money for research may come from personal savings. But major research is now too expensive for ordinary people to fund from private means. It needs big money from government, private research foundations, drug companies or rich philanthropists.

Getting money for research involves writing research proposals and applying for grants. If you intend to do serious research you should:

- talk to professional researchers for career advice
- learn how to write winning research proposals
- find potential sources of funding for your research
- learn to handle interviews for research grants.

9.4 Planning Research

Many students and young doctors, ask for help in doing research before they have identified a intriguing / important problem they wish to pursue.

James Mitchell had always been interested in research. However he had failed to secure a research registrar post. He mentioned his interest during his initial interview with Dr Judith Hughes, college tutor in paediatrics.

"What would you like to research?"

"Atypical pneumonia. What proportion of pneumonia in children is caused by mycoplasma?" James replied.

"What is the importance of knowing the incidence of mycoplasma pneumonia?" Dr Smith probed.

"If we knew the incidence of mycoplasma pneumonia we would have a good reason for requesting serological tests for mycoplasma and treating with erythromycin or newer macrolides for at least 10 days" James replied. He was informed on the subject.

"That could be an interesting subject for research. Think about how you would go about it– ethical approval, collaborators, funding, et cetera. Let us talk about it again in 2 weeks; after the Monday ward round."

Planning research means more than getting ideas. What should be done depends on the research question. Research on **humans** and **animals** *requires **approval*** from research governing bodies.

Studies on **human** subjects require **informed consent** from the individuals or somebody acting for them **before** the research can start.

In the UK clinical research can only proceed **after approval** from a **'research ethics committee'** and the NHS trust's **research and development committee**.

The process can be protracted. The primary concern of an ethics committee is patient safety. It wants reassuring answers to a few basic questions before granting approval:

- How will the patient's welfare be protected?
- Is the research likely to be clinically important to society?
- Is it primary research or a repetition of other peoples' work?

Before starting the research you must have approval from the Research and Development Committee of the trust in which patients involved in the study would be treated. The trust needs to be satisfied that patient safety will not be compromised. It might provide human and financial support for the project.

If you are interested in clinical research, you should find out where and when the local Ethics Committee meets and the membership. Get a copy of the committee's research guidelines and study them before committing yourself to a piece of research.

9.5. Doing research

Details of research are beyond the remit of this book. The local university library should have books on medical research. The chairman of the trust research committee should be able to point you in the right direction.

Does your research require:
- laboratory experiments (permits, equipment, materials, assistants...)?
- human subjects (informed consent, approval by Ethics Committee...)?
- live animal studies (Home Office approval, animal rightists issues...)?
- interviewing people (assistants, questionnaires, interpreters...)?

These and many other issues must be considered and solved before the study begins. Politeness and humility are essential in medical and sociological research. *"Please"* and *"thank you"* are essential research tools.

James obtained and read research guidelines from the local ethical committee. After discussing the subject with Dr Hughes he decided to apply for approval for **"Incidence of mycoplasma infection in children with pneumonia"** *admitted to Catsford Infirmary.*

James was lucky. The hospital's consultant microbiologist was sympathetic. An SpR in microbiology was investigating the use of serologic tests in diagnosing pneumonias in children. Maybe the two SpRs could work together to their mutual benefit.

Michael Hodgkin, the microbiology SpR, was happy to collaborate. A consultant radiologist with an interest in paediatric radiology agreed to review chest X-ray films.

Fellow SpRs and SHOs in paediatrics agreed to help in getting informed consent, collecting epidemiological data and blood samples. The local ethical committee approved the study after only a three month wait.

Nursing staff would help by reassuring parents that the blood test would help in deciding the right antibiotic for the child and for how longer to give it.

James and his collaborators:
- *obtained informed consent from parents or guardians of children with pneumonia for collection of epidemiologic data, and blood samples and tests and clinical observations*

- *gathered epidemiologic data (age, sex, symptomatic siblings, school or nursery attendance, symptomatic classmates, etc.) on children aged 2 and 10 years. Laboratory records indicated that mycoplasma infection was most likely in that age group.*

- *collected blood samples from children with respiratory symptoms– cough, fever ≥ 38°C; and respiratory signs– crackles and pneumonic changes on chest X-rays.*

- *tested blood samples for mycoplasma IgM antibody soon after collection and gave erythromycin for 10 days to children whose sera had mycoplasma IgM.*

Over 12 months the researchers gathered data and collected blood samples from 89 children. From the ward admissions book, James estimated that another 22 could have been recruited had SpRs and SHO been as diligent at weekends as they were in weekdays.

9.6 Analysing data

Some research findings are easy to quantify and others are not. Most socio-medical studies are more interesting when their qualitative (flavour) as well as quantitative trends are reported. The style of analysis and reporting depends on the primary question.

*James' study of the "**Incidence of mycoplasma pneumonia in children**" required no statistical analysis– the numbers were small. He calculated the proportion of children with fever and respiratory symptoms whose sera had IgM antibodies to mycoplasma pneumoniae.*
* *mycoplasma IgM was detected in **x**% of samples analysed*
* *infants were less likely than toddlers to have mycoplasma IgM.*
* *mycoplasma infection was highest in children aged 2 - 4 years.*

James and Michael wrote up their findings in papers which were:
* *presented at hospital annual research meeting*
* *submitted for publications in peer reviewed journals*
* *presented at national microbiology and paediatric conferences.*

Benefits of the study
James and his collaborators will cite the study under "research", "presentation" and "publications" in their CVs– a deserved rich harvest!

Following the study, the department of microbiology agreed to routine serologic tests for mycoplasma IgM. Paediatricians persuaded to use macrolides for at least 10 days to treat mycoplasma pneumonia.

9.7 Writing the research paper

Research papers follow an **IMRD** format– *Introduction, Methods, Results, Discussion*. Study journals in your library and note how authors wrote the various sections of their papers.

Important discoveries have, however, been reported in letters to editors of journals. The structure of deoxyribonucleic acid (DNA), the genetic code, was reported by Watson and Crick in a letter in *The Lancet.*

9.7.1 The title of the paper

The title should encapsulate the research subject and its findings. It should be short, relevant, informative, and memorable. *Incidence of mycoplasma pneumonia in children* would be good for Dr Mitchell's paper.

9.7.2 Abstract

Although it follows the title, the abstract (summary) is written last. It gives a summary of the objective, methods, findings and conclusions of the study. It should capture the essence of the paper.

Incidence of mycoplasma pneumonia in children.
James Mitchell, Michael Hodgkin et al. Catsford Infirmary, Catsford.

Abstract
Objective: To determine the incidence of mycoplasma IgM in sera of children hospitalised with pneumonia.

Subjects and methods. Sera from children with cough, fever ≥ 38°C, crackles and pneumonic changes on chest X-ray were tested for mycoplasma IgM..

Results: Over 12 months sera from 89 children with pneumonia were collected and tested for mycoplasma IgM antibodies. **x**% of sera contained mycoplasma IgM. The incidence of mycoplasma pneumonia was highest in 2 - 4 year old children.

Conclusion: An **x**% incidence of mycoplasma pneumonia justifies routine serologic tests for and the use of macrolide for at least 10 days.

Abstracts may be written in different formats. Some journals use subheadings, others omit them and the text merges into a solid paragraph. I prefer those with subheadings; they are easier to read. Many doctors read the abstract first and only when they find it interesting or relevant to their practice do they read the rest of the article.

9.7.3 Introduction
- Why was the study done?
- What were you looking for?

James was intrigued by the morbidity associated with mycoplasma pneumonia and wanted to know how common the disease was.

9.7.4 Methods (including subjects and materials)
What did you study?
James studied the presence of mycoplasma IgM in sera of children with pneumonia.

How did you do it?
With colleagues, he collected epidemiological data and blood samples on children aged 2- 10 years with fever, respiratory symptoms and pneumonia changes on chest X-rays. The sera were analysed for mycoplasma IgM.

9.7.5 Results (findings)
What did you find?
The study found that x% of children with respiratory symptoms and fever had mycoplasma IgM.

Statistical analysis
Statistical analysis is necessary if controls (for subjects, intervention, etc) are used. It attempts to measure the probability (likelihood) that the observed differences occurred by chance.

James' study does not require statistical tests– calculation of percentages is enough. If the number of children tested was large he could test for statistical significance of different infection rates with age, sibling groups, school or nursery attendance, etc.

9.7.6 Discussion
- What do the findings mean?
- How do your findings compare with published studies?
- Could you have done this study better? How?

James and Mitchell discussed and compared their results with published studies on the incidence and laboratory findings in mycoplasma pneumonia. An x% incidence of mycoplasma pneumonia justifies routine serologic tests for mycoplasma pneumoniae and use of a macrolide for at least 10 days.

James criticised his study– small numbers– and suggest that a larger study would give a more accurate estimate of the incidence of mycoplasma pneumonia.

- What are your conclusions?
- What are the implications of your findings?

James' study showed that the incidence of mycoplasma pneumonia in children was high enough to justify routine serologic testing in children with respiratory symptoms and the use of macrolides for 10 days.

- What should be done next?
Sera from children in whom mycoplasma pneumonia is suspected should tested for mycoplasma IgM, and macrolide used for 10 days.

9.7.9 References
At the end of a paper the author lists papers and books cited in the article. References enable readers to search for, and read texts that have been quoted. Follow the Vancouver format for citing references:

Citing a book:
Yate M. **The Ultimate CV Book:** *write the perfect CV and get that job*
London: Kogan Page 2003.

Citing a journal article:
International Committee of Medical Journal Editors. **Uniform Requirements for manuscripts submitted to Biomedical Journals.** *Ann Inter Med* 1997; 126: 36-47.

Citing a report:
Commons Select Committee on Health. **Patient and Public Involvement in the NHS.** 7th Report, July 2003. ISBN 0 21 501197 X

Citing information on the internet:
http://www.cppih.org/ppi_new.html Patient and Public Involvement (PPI) Forum (accessed 13 February 2004)

Do not misquote any publication to give false support to your research. You risk being found out and disgraced in the same journal.

Summary

• Think careful about your research question. Is it exciting?

• Identify resources (personal funds, research grants and time)

• Obtain approvals from relevant bodies (Home Office for animals studies, Ethics Committee and Trust's Research and Development Committee for clinical research) before committing resources.

• Plan your study with its analysis in mind; sample size, controls, inclusion and exclusion, etc. Have you asked "why, how, when" for insight into the qualitative aspect of your research?

Writing the medical CV

- Analyse your data:
  Has the research answered your question?
  What are the main findings of your study?
  What is the meaning of your results?
  Are your findings statistically significant?

- What are the deficits of the study? How would you correct them?

Find a publisher for your paper. Send dissertation to examiners.

Further Reading

1. Bowling A. **Research Methods in Health**. Oxford: OUP 2002

2. Calnan J. **Coping with Research- *The complete Guide for Beginners***. London: Heinemann 1984.

3. Campbell M. **Statistics at square one.** London: BMJ Books 2002

4. International Committee of Medical Journal Editors. **Uniform Requirements for manuscripts submitted to Biomedical Journals.** *Ann Inter Med* 1997; 126: 36-47.

---

10. Dissertation/ thesis

Dissertation/ thesis

10.1 Need for a higher degree

Perhaps you would like to enhance the impact of your CV by studying for, and acquiring a higher degree. Congratulations. You will miss a lot of TV, read a lot of waffle, and learn how to type (sorry, acquire keyboard skills!).

In pursuit of a higher university degree, may be an MSc, a ChM/ MS, an MD or a PhD, you will be required to write a dissertation or thesis. You will be guided by a supervisor and the thesis will be scrutinised by university examiners. Some universities hold oral examinations (viva voce) on dissertations/ theses.

If your dissertation, like other requirements before it, is successful you will receive you degree. If unsuccessful, you will have spent money, time and labour, and missed much TV– but maybe wiser.

10.2. What is a dissertation/thesis?

A dissertation (thesis) is an academic monograph (small A4 book) prepared on the lines of a research paper, but more thorough. It is written at the behest of a university for the requirements of a diploma or degree– MSc, MD, PhD or other.

Dissertation = critique, thesis, discourse, essay, exposition, treatise, etc.
Thesis = treatise, dissertation, essay, monograph, hypothesis, etc.

Discourses for Diplomas and some Master's degrees are usually called dissertations, while those for most Master's, MD and PhD degrees are called theses.

Now that you know the difference between *dissertation and thesis,* let us, for the purposes of this discussion, assume that *dissertation = thesis.*

10.3 Supervisors

Preparing a dissertation for a higher degree begins with registration as a student at a university. This is followed by assignment of a supervisor before the research for the dissertation/thesis can start. Ideas for research and the dissertation are discussed with and agreed by the supervisor.

The supervisor decides if and when, the research, and later the dissertation are progressing satisfactorily. He/she decides if and when the student may submit the dissertation to examiners and therefore if and when the student gets the degree!

10.5 Structure of a dissertation

The structure of a dissertation is the same as that used for audits and research papers. The monograph is given a title on a title page, a summary, list of contents, a list of references and an appendix or appendices.

- **Title page** (with the title of dissertation, author(s) names, a phrase specified by the institution and the date of submission to examiners
- **Summary** of the dissertation *(a few to several pages)*
- **List of contents** and the pages they start on *(one to a few pages)*
- **Introduction** *(a number of pages)*
- **Methods** *(pages to a short chapter)*
- **Results** *(one or a few chapters)*
- **Discussion** *(pages to a chapter)*
- **Conclusions** *(a page or two)*
- **Recommendations** *(a page or two)*
- **References** (bibliography) *(one to several pages)*
- **Appendices** *(a number of pages).*

If you are about to write a dissertation you should examine samples of successful dissertations in your college or university library.

Study the dissertation for:
- structure and layout (format)
- the language (style and grammar)
- use of tables, figures and quotations
- depth and sophistication of exposition
- the *'finish'* (production) and quality of the *book.*

Select two you consider the best, study them closely and appreciate the attributes of a successful dissertation. When you write your own, do not copy the language of any particular thesis. Write it your way.

10.4 Length of a dissertation

It is the quality of your research, the detail and relevance of the data, the thoroughness of your analysis, the style and language of your writing that matter and not the number of pages or weight *(pounds, kilograms)* of the *book.*

Most universities indicate the expected size of the dissertation in number of words (between *x* and *x+n* words long). So you should know how longer your dissertation should be. Some candidates find it difficult to make the minimum while other others can edit their work down to the maximum number of words.

While a paper may be a few pages long, the length of a dissertation varies from under, to well over, one hundred pages long. Some sections may be several pages long, while others may need division into chapters. The *Results* section is often a few chapters long. However a dissertation requires more than length.

A thesis is supposed to be more thorough than a dissertation. However some dissertations are quite good, sometimes better than some theses. Your university will has copies of successful dissertations from past students for you to examine. Follow your university's requirements for diplomas and higher degrees. Get a copy of the university's regulations and guidelines for writing dissertations/theses early.

10.6 Tone of dissertation

What will be the tone of your dissertation? Journals, reports and dissertations are usually written in the *third person singular.* It is claimed that this encourages objectivity.

Third person singular:
The author studied mating habits of 124 kites...

First person singular:
I studied mating habits of 124 kites...

How does the use of a phrase *"the author"* instead of "**I**" or "**We**", enhances objectivity? The claim to objectivity is false. One can be as subjective (biased) in the *third* as in the *first person singular.*

The third person singular produces clumsy prose. Repeating *"the author"* is tedious; a simple (and humble) *"I"* would suffice. Fortunately there is a welcome tendency to use *I* and *We* in academic writing.

Find out what your university (and therefore examiners) recommend and use that. After graduation you may use whichever voice you like.

10.7. Watch your language

Spelling and grammar may decide the outcome of you dissertation. If your thesis reads well, the spelling and grammar are correct, your examiners will be more likely to award marks more readily. Irritate them with poor spelling, grating grammar and you make them mean (stingy) with marks.

Writing the medical CV

Your thesis should say what you want it to say; no more, no less
- think of what you want to say and how you will say it
- avoid ambiguity, your arguments should be clearly understood
- use clear simple words, avoid jargon wherever possible
- use short words, short sentences, and short paragraphs
- be methodical, tell the story sequentially
- avoid superfluous words and phrases
- avoid the urge to impress. Just write well.

Your thesis should be written in an active language. Emphasise the action of the methods, results, technical analysis *(with statistics if relevant),* discussion and conclusion.

10.8 Submitting your dissertation
Universities have rules about preparing dissertations (general format, mandatory statements on the title page, word spacing and binding).
- Follow your university's regulations
- Respect your supervisor's advice on the quality of your research
- Listen to your supervisor's comments and advice on your writing
- Leave time for remedial work *(research, literature reviews, rewrites..)*
- Sort out practical details (typing, binding, number of copies?) early
- Check the grammar– read what you have written. Spellcheckers still have difficulties with grammar.

When you and your supervisor are happy with the dissertation, produce and submit the right number of copies for examiners, and wait. You can now complete the clinical audit.

10.9 Defending your dissertation
Some universities hold oral examinations (viva voce) on theses. In the Viva the candidate is questioned about her/his dissertation as part of the requirements for the degree. Usually two *inquisitors,* maybe more, examine candidates.

Know your dissertation, and be ready to defend it from attack. Legend has it that several centuries ago, PhD candidates were examined in the town hall. There, they publicly defended their theses. If successful, they were thereafter addressed as *'doctor'*. *Doctor* originally meant learned person, teacher!

Be prepared to discuss the *why, how, and what* of your dissertation:

- why did you do the research/study?
- why did you do it that way?
- what does the literature say on the subject?
- what did you find?
- what do your findings mean?
- how do you explain your results?
- what should be done next?

What are the weaknesses of your research?
What the weaknesses in your analyses?
How would you correct them?

Good luck with the examiners.

Have you 'examined' your dissertation for spelling and grammatical mistakes?

Summary

- A dissertation is mandatory for most higher university degrees. It is usually based on a piece of research.

- A dissertation is an academic monograph on the lines of a research paper, but much longer and more thorough in exposition and detail.

- Supervisors are essential in the research and writing of dissertations. They decide if the research and dissertation are progressing satisfactorily and when you submit the dissertation to examiners.
- Spelling and grammar may decide the outcome of you dissertation.

Writing the medical CV

Irritate examiners with poor spelling, grating grammar and you make them mean (stingy) in awarding marks.

* The dissertation is given a title on a title page, a list of contents, a summary, a body (the real dissertation), a list of references, appendices, and neat binding before it is ready for examiners' eyes.

* Follow your university's rules on typing, number of words, layout of title page, production (of the book) and numbers of copies to submit.

* If required, prepare well for the Viva (the inquisition)– the defence of your dissertation.

Will you show us the Graduation Video?

Further Reading

1. Bowling A. **Research Methods in Health**. Oxford: Oxford University Press 2002.

2. Calnan J. **Coping with Research-** *The complete Guide for Beginners*. London: Heinemann 1984.

3. Watson G. **Writing a Thesis–** *a guide to long essays and dissertations*. London: Longman 1987.

4. Albert T. **A - Z of Medical Writing.** London: *BMJ* Books 2000

5. Ritter RM. **The Oxford Manual of Style**. Oxford: Oxford University Press 2002.

6. Luey B. **Handbook for Academic Authors.** Cambridge: Cambridge University Press 2002.

Index

Glossary (of unusual abbreviations)

BCG = Bacillus Calmette-Guerin (a vaccine against tuberculosis)

CCST = certificate of completion of specialist training

CEO = chief executive officer (head of an organisation)

LAS = locum appointment service

LAT = locum appointment training

MBA = masters in business administration

MDU = medical defence union

MPS = medical protection society

OSCE= objective structured clinical exam

PLAB = preliminary language and assessment board

PRO = public relations officer

RITA = Record of In-Training Assessment

Comments on "**Writing the medical CV**"

If you have comments on:
- How the book could be improved, or
- Subjects to include in next edition…

Please contact:
Sam McErin at <u>sammcerin@yahoo.co.uk</u>

Create your success

You won't try in case you fail?
You can't win unless you try!
You must strive to succeed

Dreams, goals of your imagination
Nourish and direct your enterprise
To build a future to your ambition

Nirvana without faith is unattainable
Reward without labour uneconomic
Success without goals impossible

Celebrate your proud creation
Triumph from resolute execution
Of dreams, goals and targets set.